Pony & Rider
Book

Pony & Rider

Book

The
Warwick
Press

Acknowledgements

The publishers gladly acknowledge the owners and copyright holders of photographs reproduced in the book. We hope that any inadvertently omitted from this list will accept a general acknowledgement.

Australian Information Service: 141; A. S. Barnes: 148; John Elliot: title page, 23 (below), 51 (top), 95; Candida Hunt: 46 (right), 47 (foot), 57, 65, 68, 74, 114 (below, right); Peter Landon: 55, 70 (below); Leslie Lane: 13 (left), 14 (both), 17 (top), 20, 107, 129, 136, 152–3; A. C. Littlejohns: 137 (top); Frank H. Meads: 145; Monty: 121 (right); Norwegian Embassy: 24 (foot); Peter Phillips: 30 (top), 34, 38, 43, 63, 70, 75, 114 (left), 115 (right); Picturepoint: 142; Riding Magazine: 53; Mike Roberts: 146; Peter Roberts: 9, 10 (top), 11 (both), 12, 13 (right), 16, 19, 28, 52, 82, 83, 99, 108, 110, 119, 120 (below), 122, 123, 125 (left), 130, 131, 134 (below), 135 (below), 143, 151; Scottish Tourist Board: 27; Spectrum: 15; Bob Targett: 35 (right), 41, 46 (left), 47 (top), 51 (below), 78, 86, 87, 90, 91, 92, 98, 102, 106, 114 (top and centre), 115 (top and centre); Sally Anne Thompson: 22, 23 (top); United Press, Paris: 150 (below).

Cover illustrations:
Front: Debbie Johnsey (photograph Peter Roberts)
Back: photograph Sally Anne Thompson

ISBN 0 7063 4112 0

First published in Great Britain in 1977
by Ward Lock Limited, 82 Gower Street,
London WC1E 6EQ, a Pentos company.

Reprinted in 1979, 1982

House editor: Eleanor-Mary Cadell

Layout by Sheila Sherwen

Cover designed by Graham Mitchener

Text filmset in Baskerville
by Amos Typesetters, Hockley, Essex.

Printed and bound by
Toppan Printing Co., Singapore.

Contents

Introduction

Opinions vary on the question of intelligence in ponies. Some people maintain that they are very simple-minded animals, largely dependent on instinct, impulse and the discipline imposed upon them by human beings. Others credit them with a high IQ, but the truth lies somewhere in between and to understand a pony one has to take account of both its anatomy and its origins.

In nature vegetarian animals have always been hunted by meat-eating animals. This meant that a grazing wild horse had to keep a constant look-out for fear of attack by perhaps a tiger or wolves, and was better able to do this by having a wide range of vision which allowed it to see what was happening on either flank. So all animals that are naturally hunted have eyes in the sides of their faces, which focus independently of each other to give a broad picture of their surroundings; whereas the hunter, the tiger or whatever it may be, is interested only in its prey and needs to focus accurately on that in order to creep up on it and catch it. For this reason, meat-eating animals have their eyes set forward.

It takes some effort to imagine what the world would seem like if your ears were on top of your head, capable of various movements that enabled you to catch tiny sounds, while your eyes were in the side of your head, seeing all sorts of things at once in two sideways views, but with a fairly broad blank space in the area immediately in front of your long nose and jaw. This unsighted area causes a pony to lift and turn its head sharply if you put a hand up directly between its eyes, because it is unable to see what you are going to do.

If you add to these differences a very highly developed sense of smell, which would allow you to catch minute air-borne scents or to sort out from a bundle of hay a particularly tasty leaf, you are getting somewhere near being a pony, who has been born with an inherited instinct to react quickly to unfamiliar sights, sounds and smells from wild ancestors whose survival depended on it. Then you begin to realize that it is not stupidity that makes a pony shy at a sack lying beside the road, and to appreciate the remarkable degree of trust and intelligence which is shown by a police horse trained to walk through banner-waving crowds, regardless of shouting, pistol shots and even a burning fire.

Animals are very limited in their means of communication with each other by

7

voice. Ponies squeal with anger or, in the case of mares, flirtatiously; they whinny friendly greetings and give loud neighs to say, 'Here am I, where are you?'; otherwise they depend on signals such as laid-back ears to tell them that a companion is unfriendly and liable to kick or bite, and to some degree on sensing the intentions of others.

As your pony gets to know you, it soon learns to read signs that tell it that you are pleased, cross or nervous, and it will tend to behave accordingly. This is why a normally well-mannered pony will sometimes disgrace itself in a situation that has made its rider apprehensive – for example, hunting or entering a show for the first time. This is one good reason for remaining kind, firm and calm with a pony in all circumstances, making it clear that while it is your pride and joy, you will not stand any nonsense and everything is entirely under your control. People who handle ponies like this generally have very happy, well-disciplined ones of which they can be proud.

1 Ponies of the world

Ponies of the British Isles

The British Isles has a unique place in the world as the birthplace of more breeds of pony than any other single country. All these descend from the primitive types of horse that roamed wild in prehistoric times. Britain was then joined to the continent of Europe by a land bridge and the Channel was a great river valley. In the course of time the land bridge was eroded to isolate these islands with a stock of wild horses and these developed into distinct breeds according to where they lived and their domesticated use by man over a period of several thousand years. This has left us a heritage of ponies, some, like the Exmoor, resembling their Celtic ancestors and others, such as the Welsh and New Forest breeds, showing the influence of Arabian blood, which was introduced during the past few hundred years.

Connemara pony

The Connemara is a native breed confined to an area of the west coast of southern Ireland, where it has lived since time immemorial. It is thought that at some time in the past it was improved by the addition of Arab or Spanish blood, traditionally from a few horses saved from an Armada wreck but, in reality, it is more likely that the animals were traded by Spanish and Irish merchants. This pony is hardy and strong, docile and intelligent. Some years ago the commonest colour was dun, but this is now rare and Connemaras are usually grey, black, bay or brown, with a chestnut or roan appearing occasionally. It is a sturdy animal with short legs and a longish body, and tremendous bone. The height is between 13 and 14.2 hands. The breed society in Britain is the English Connemara Pony Society.

Ireland's only surviving pony breed, the Connemara. This pretty foal should make a good riding pony.

Dales pony

Similar to the Fell in some respects, the Dales pony is found mainly in Northumberland and Durham, east of the Pennines. The largest and strongest of the native pony breeds, it used to be employed in farm work, but is now popular as a trekking pony. Although sturdy, the Dales has a neat 'pony' head and compact body with good straight action. The most common colours are black, grey and brown, but greys are also permitted. Height: not to exceed 14.2 hands. The breed society is the Dales Pony Society.

Above: A Connemara mare enjoys the lush spring pasture.

Below: The Connemara Pony Show which is held at Clifden, County Galway, each year in August.

Map showing areas of British native breeds of pony.

Above and below: Dartmoor ponies need their qualities of hardiness and surefootedness in order to survive in the harsh moorland environment.

Dartmoor pony

This is an ancient breed that has somehow continued to survive in one of the toughest areas of England, where it must dig in the snow to live during the winter. Yet, a true Dartmoor is an elegant pony with a lot of presence, and, properly handled, makes an ideal first pony for a child. Any colour is allowed except skewbald and piebald, and the height is up to 12.2 hands. Even nowadays these ponies are ridden by moormen tending their herds and flocks, and earlier this century they were still used for work in tin mines; a use that nearly resulted in the total loss of the pure Dartmoor, when short-sighted owners of moorland stock introduced Shetland stallions to make ponies destined for the mines smaller and so handier for the purpose. Fortunately, the Dartmoor Pony Society, supported by the British Horse Society and a number of breeders, stepped in to ensure the continuation of the breed, but most of the best Dartmoor ponies are bred away from the moor which is now, sadly, populated by numerous scraggy mongrels.

Exmoor pony

These ponies are native to the area of moor that lies across north Devon and Somerset and are believed to be of pure and ancient lineage, owing nothing to any breed other than the original wild horse of early Britain. An Exmoor is easily recognized by its unique 'mealy' markings on the muzzle and round the eyes (so-called 'toad eye'); it is also limited to three colours, namely bay, brown or dun, with black points, and no white markings are permitted. Height: adult stallions may be up to 12.3 hands and mares 12.2 hands. The Exmoor is hardy and agile, strongly built, with an extra-thick winter coat to help it to withstand the harsh climate of the moors. If they are taken in hand at a young age, Exmoor ponies make very good family ponies and are lovable characters, but animals broken at a later stage can be wild and intractable. Unlike the Dartmoor, the best still roam the moors and some of these can be seen at Bampton Fair in Devon, where they are brought for sale after the annual round-up.

Fell pony

This is another type that is distinct and recognizable; in this case by its full, rather curly mane and tail and well-feathered heels. It is a native of the moors of northern England where it was used mainly as a pack-pony, and for this reason it is a very powerful animal for its size, excelling in bone. The most popular colour is whole-black, but it may be dark brown, dark bay and, rarely, grey or dun. Height: about 13.2 hands. In recent years these ponies have become popular for riding and are, indeed, good all-rounders of a useful size. The breed society is the Fell Pony Society.

Opposite: Three handsome Exmoor ponies in their native setting.

Above, left and above: Two Exmoor champions, with their characteristic mealy markings on the muzzle and round the eyes.

Left: A sturdy Fell, ideal for trekking and long-distance riding. This versatile pony can easily carry an adult.

13

Above: Semi-wild Highland ponies on the Scottish hills.

Below: A Highland stallion outlined against the sky shows a neat head, powerfully muscular body and short strong legs.

Highland pony

There are two types of Highland pony, depending on where they are found rather than on any real difference. Those from the Western Isles are the smallest (12.2 to 13.2 hands); while the so-called 'Mainland' pony is the largest of the British mountain and moorland breeds and averages 14.2 hands. The Highland is very strong and docile and makes a pleasant ride for hacking or trekking but, as its natural pace is walking or trotting, tends to be uncomfortable when asked for more speed; this is in spite of the fact that, in common with so many other breeds, it has a dash of Arab in its ancestry. It is a handsome, kind-natured pony of good conformation and is becoming increasingly popular in England. The colour may be black, brown, grey or dun with no markings but, generally, a dark 'eel stripe' along the ridge of the back; and a further colour is bright chestnut with silver mane and tail, which is, obviously, prized for its spectacular effect. The breed society is the Highland Pony Society.

New Forest pony

Ponies wandered in the New Forest in Saxon times but in the course of history various stallions were introduced, including Arabs and Thoroughbreds, so that the present-day animal may be considered as a composite that has developed a definite type, largely due to its environment. It might be thought that in the pleasant south of England protected by a huge forest, life would be easy for these ponies, but the reverse is true, for the grazing is meagre and hard to find during

A New Forest mare and foal grazing in the peace of the Forest.

Above: A champion New Forest stallion. Most of these ponies still run loose in the Forest, but the stallions are inspected for quality every year and a high standard of breeding is maintained.

Opposite, top: A champion riding pony, Holly of Shring.

Opposite, below: Shetlands, the smallest pony breed. Their double winter coat, profuse mane and thick, long tail give them some protection in the cold and wet winter climate.

the winter, and survival depends on stamina, since a foal must live amongst rough ground, bogs and high heather. The result in the best specimens is a thoroughbred air combined with toughness, and such animals have been the foundation of many successful show-pony studs. Any colour is permitted but brown and bay is most common; while the height is the most varied of any breed, being between 12 and 14.2 hands. The breed is controlled by the New Forest Pony Breeding and Cattle Society.

Riding pony

Another composite animal carrying the blood of two or more breeds usually a cross between one of the native pony breeds and a small Thoroughbred or Arab. This combination achieves a type of pony excelling in conformation and suitability as a child's hunter and show pony. They are often of Welsh New Forest and Dartmoor extraction, the most popular being the Welsh Mountain. Height is generally between 13 and 14.2 hands, but the show ring makes allowance for small ponies. There are three heights of classes: under 12.2 hands; 12.2 to 13.2 hands; and 13.2 to 14.2 hands. These ponies are registered with the National Pony Society.

Shetland pony

The Shetland is in a class by itself; a tough little creature hailing from the far north – the Shetland and Orkney Islands – but now known all over the world,

Above: A herd of Welsh ponies on the Welsh hills.

Opposite: A Palomino Welsh Mountain pony.

mainly as a pet although in its native islands it works hard for a living. They are not suitable for cross-breeding, as their disastrous use on Dartmoor has shown, but many people own Shetland studs for the pleasure of keeping these charming ponies, which make docile mounts for small children and, in recent years, they have become popular in harness – doing well in driving classes at several major shows. Registered Shetlands must not exceed 42 inches when full grown. Any colour is allowed. The breed society is the Shetland Pony Stud Book Society.

Welsh ponies

Most people would agree that the Welsh Mountain pony and the Welsh Riding pony are the most beautiful of the mountain and moorland breeds. Ponies have lived in wild Wales for many centuries, enduring great hardship both in their natural environment and as working pit ponies, besides carrying farmers over the hills and pulling tradesmen's carts. This has required and produced stamina and intelligence of a high order. The Welsh breed has been divided into four sections which are registered as Section A (Welsh Mountain); Section B (Welsh Riding); Section C (Welsh Pony Cob); and Section D (Welsh Cob, of draught type). All are registered with the Welsh Pony and Cob Society.

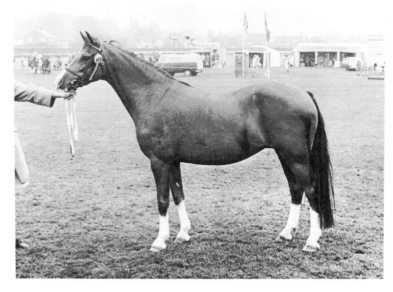

Top, left and right: Welsh Mountain ponies, sections A and B.

Above: Welsh, section C, combines pony characteristics with robustness and substance.

Above, right: Fine action from a Welsh Cob (section D) in harness.

Section A The appearance of a Welsh Mountain pony suggests an Arab in miniature and it has the same style. This makes it a popular show pony in riding, in-hand and leading-rein classes, and also, usually in pairs, in driving classes. Its action is fast, free and straight from the shoulder, which is spectacular at an extended trot. This asset led to its use in the development of the Hackney pony. Any colour except pie – or skewbald – is allowed, and this applies to all the Welsh strains. 'Wall' (blue) eyes are permitted. Height: 12 hands.

Section B This is a larger version, known as the Welsh Riding pony, which may be rather sturdier in build but with all the quality of its small relative. Height: not to exceed 13.2 hands.

Section C Larger again and 'cobbier', that is, sturdier and more powerful; but still retaining the small head and general style of the last two. It is, also, an ancestor of Hackney and Trotting horses. Its strength and reliable nature make it an ideal pony for trekking. Height: about 14.2 hands.

Section D The Welsh Cob usually exceeds the official pony maximum of 14.2 hands although it belongs to the same breed society. It combines a large body and short, powerful legs with an elegant head and balanced action. With a natural jumping ability and a determined temperament, this type makes an excellent hunter. Height: 14.2 to 15.1 hands.

Ponies of Europe, Asia and Australia

While British ponies are known and valued in many parts of the world, breeds from other countries are seldom seen outside their boundaries. Those of Northern Europe are, largely, of the same basic type as the Norwegian Fjord Pony, suited to hard work and a rigorous climate. In warmer parts where Europe and southern Asia merge some native breeds, such as the Caspian, have been refined to a more Arabian type – perhaps due to the introduction of Arab blood or because they descend from the same root stock.

Caspian pony
A native of the shores of the Caspian Sea in Northern Iran, this tiny pony can be traced back as far as 3,000 BC and is probably the forerunner of most of the hot-blooded breeds of horse known today. This pony was virtually rediscovered in Iran in 1965 and now several have been imported into Britain. Caspian stallions crossed with Welsh mares have produced some beautiful show ponies. They are small, narrow ponies, with a kindly temperament, ideal for children, and are capable of great speed and good jumping ability. Colours are bay, or grey and chestnut, with occasional white markings on head and legs. True 'hot-bloods', they are best described as miniature Thoroughbreds, measuring between 11 and 12 hands. Pure and half-breds are registered with The British Caspian Society.

Haflinger pony
This is a native of the Austrian Tyrol, carefully bred for strength and surefootedness, which has made it invaluable as a pack and draught animal in a mountainous area. A few have been brought to Britain in recent years and may be seen in driving classes and as ridden ponies at shows. It is of similar type to the English Fell pony; always chestnut with a flaxen mane and tail, standing just under 14 hands. They are registered with the Haflinger Society.

21

Above: Good, free action in a two-year-old Caspian stallion.
Opposite: A Caspian mare with her week-old colt foal.

Below: A fine Haflinger stallion, Maximilian, imported from Austria and the first stallion to be registered with the British Haflinger Society.

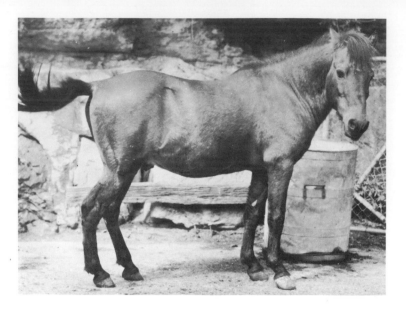

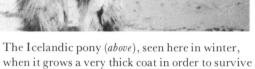

The Icelandic pony (*above*), seen here in winter, when it grows a very thick coat in order to survive the harsh conditions of the northern climate.

Top right: The Timor pony, a small but high-spirited animal.

Right and below: Norwegian Fjord ponies, used as draught animals for farm work, and in the wild.

Iceland pony

Ponies were taken to Iceland by the first Scandinavian settlers more than a thousand years ago, where they were used as pack and riding ponies, as meat at feasts and in the then-popular sport of horse-fighting. In the course of centuries a definite type developed with the addition of imports from Ireland: it is a stocky animal with a large head set on a short, thick neck, and a heavy mane and forelock. The height is from 12 to 13 hands. The normal pace of the Iceland pony is an ambling walk which, combined with its docile temperament, has made it ideal for trekking holidays.

Mongolian pony

A descendant of the Przewalski horse (one of the ancestors of our present-day breeds), this sturdy pack-pony is found all over Mongolia, Tibet and China. It is capable of great speed over short distances, as well as endurance in its draught work for the nomadic herdsmen. Height: usually about 13 to 14 hands. Colours are black, brown, bay or various shades of dun.

Norwegian Fjord pony

These are powerful little animals of a primitive but most attractive type, kept on farms and smallholdings in many parts of Scandinavia for draught purposes. Since this pony is descended from the same ancestral stock, it resembles the Iceland breed in general size and conformation, but is distinguished by its colour, which may be described as a creamy dun. The legs are dark and some show zebra markings. All have an eel-stripe running through the mane to the tail and the mane is usually clipped to stand up in a crest with the dark centre showing above the light side hairs. It moves well at a brisk trot, and is becoming known outside its native area as the popularity of driving grows.

Timor pony

This pony is a native of the Island of Timor in the Indian Ocean, off the north-west coast of Australia. Because of their remarkable hardiness and stamina they were imported into Western Australia in the nineteenth century, and their influence later spread throughout the Australian mainland. They are usually dark in colour, and extremely agile for their small size of about 12 hands.

2 Where you can ride without owning a pony

The most obvious and probably the best way to start riding is to arrange for a series of lessons at a riding school. To find a suitable school in your area, ask for advice from local people who are experienced riders or from a veterinary surgeon, or, failing that, resort to looking under the appropriate heading in the Yellow Pages directory. Both the British Horse Society and the Association of British Riding Schools provide lists of approved establishments, and these can be obtained on request.

Without other guidance it is possible to judge a school on three basic principles: the proprietor and the instructors must be qualified, the stables clean and tidy, and the ponies well fed, groomed and shod. All this can be discovered on a preliminary visit to the stables when, assuming that the school reaches the required standard, lessons may be arranged.

Some riding schools will accept part-time unpaid help in the stables and this is a good way to learn how to handle and groom ponies and how to muck out properly. But such arrangements are a success only if the helper is really prepared to work, and if the staff will vary the jobs so that it is not just an hour or so of toiling to and from the dung heap with a wheelbarrow. An occasional free ride or a reduction in tuition fees is sometimes given in return for work, but, generally, doing odd jobs about the stables is considered part of learning and this is, essentially, true.

As a rule, lessons are given on an hourly basis. You will start by learning how to mount and dismount correctly; how to hold the reins and sit down in the saddle with the correct length of stirrup; and then progress through conveying your wishes to the pony by means of the 'aids' to the rising trot, canter and gallop. After digesting these lessons you will have arrived at the point where you seldom fall off without a reasonable excuse, and have enough confidence to ride out alone on a well-behaved pony. Most people will wish to take further lessons in jumping.

Not all riding schools are prepared to hire out ponies but some will, particularly to their own pupils. The alternative is a livery stable, but here again the choice should be made carefully as, otherwise, you may end up with a sullen 'slug' of a pony or, worse, one that proves hard-mouthed and intractable. In either case, your first solo ride will be an unhappy experience.

26

Pony trekking in the Highlands of Scotland.

Riders being trained to work over ground rails in an indoor manège, under the supervision of an instructor.

In recent years pony-trekking holidays have become popular. Most of the trekking centres are set in the more remote parts of the countryside in areas of natural beauty, where groups of riders follow a planned route each day under the guidance of one of the staff. Accommodation is provided, usually for a one- or two-week period. Since a few disreputable establishments show more interest in making money than in the welfare of their ponies, the Ponies of Britain Club has instituted controls and the registration of centres in England, Scotland and Wales. This means that only centres where the ponies and their equipment are kept in a satisfactory condition can display a Certificate of Approval; others are best avoided, because apart from poor ponies the board and lodging provided may be inadequate.

Riding tours are less commonly available than pony trekking and more expensive. This is because a tour involves overnight stops at various places along a route and this requires advance hotel bookings and arrangements for housing and feeding the animals as well; whereas a trekking party returns to base each evening. This also means that the rider needs to be fairly experienced and accustomed to riding over long distances, since the full distance between stopping-places has to be covered each day. Particulars of trekking centres and tours may be found advertised in various country and pony magazines, or

28

obtained from one of the tourist boards. Riding tours in Iceland, the United States, Australia and European countries, such as Austria and Spain, can be booked through a travel agent.

If you have somewhere to keep a pony at home, it may be possible to hire one for the summer holidays when you are knowledgeable enough to be able to ride and care for it properly, and this is quite a good scheme as a trial run before buying a pony of your own. But be sure that the pony you hire is healthy and well-mannered, and also check on the insurance position from the point of view of accidents to the animal and third-party insurance in case of accident or damage to other people or their property.

Once you are able to ride well, it may be possible to contact owners of ponies who want to enter them in show classes but lack a competent rider on some occasions. But these chances are open only when you have become expert both as a rider and in the art of showing. Even at small local shows jumping is organized under the British Show Jumping Association rules and junior events will be scheduled for ponies owned by adult members of the association and ridden by junior members.

Riding clothes

Before you ride, certain clothes are essential for your comfort and safety. The first item is a 'hard hat' – a velvet peaked cap with a reinforced crown to act as a crash-helmet in the event of a fall. While a cap is often obtainable second-hand in

Pony trekking can be a great adventure – especially when riding in the mountains of Switzerland.

29

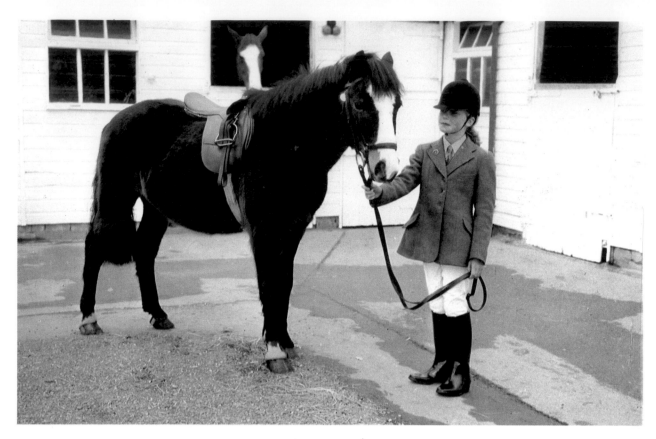

Dressed for riding. The girl in the stable yard is in semi-formal riding clothes, with riding hat and rubber riding boots. In more casual fashion, but still of course with a hard hat and suitable footwear, the girl on the left rides her Shetland pony along the beach.

good condition, having been outgrown by the first owner, it should not be a casual purchase. Iit is very important that a cap is neither too big nor too small, but fits firmly on your head without being uncomfortably tight.

Suitable footwear is next in importance. Shoes are not good as they leave the ankles unprotected and, in this case, it is worth spending a little extra on a pair of jodhpur boots, which are ankle-high and either elastic-sided or fasten with a strap. Ordinary rubber Wellington boots can be useful as an alternative, but are rather hot if worn for any length of time, and you should ensure that they have a reasonably pronounced heel or your foot could slip right through the stirrup.

What you wear between your head and your feet for everyday hacking or exercise, or on a trekking holiday, is really immaterial, provided that it is comfortable. Jeans are an obvious choice (not the flared kind) and these are now made with padding inside the leg for riding. Jodhpurs, or riding trousers, are, of course, the proper outfit and are certainly the most hard-wearing form of clothing.

Depending on the weather, a shirt and, perhaps, a tie or a polo-necked jersey may be worn, with the addition of a tweed hacking jacket or nylon anorak if necessary. Clearly, riding clothes can cost a lot of money but it is unnecessary to spend very much during the initial stages of your riding career.

3 Looking after a pony

In order to look after a pony properly you need a paddock, some form of stabling and a supply of good hay. These may seem simple requirements but it is not always so easy to persuade a farmer to let you graze a pony on his land and, when he does agree, the field may be wet or badly fenced or otherwise unsuitable. Equally, any old shed will not do as a stable because a pony needs an airy but draught-proof house with a solid floor that can be cleaned easily. Hay, on the other hand, is usually available but the problem with it is one of price and its quality must also be considered. Bearing all this in mind, anyone intent on owning a pony needs to make careful preparations before going out to buy it, which is why advice on buying your first pony is given at the end of this chapter rather than at the beginning.

The paddock

Grass is the basic food of the horse family and so a paddock is not just a place where the pony lives when it is not stabled or being ridden out, but is an enclosure of land on which it feeds, takes exercise and deposits dung. Seen in this light, it is clear that a paddock needs looking after just as much as its occupant.

Modern farming practice achieves a number of different kinds of grass fields: many are ploughed regularly and sown with special mixtures of grasses and clover to provide rich food for cattle, which suits them but is not good for ponies because some of the plants involved make them too fat and liable to inflammation in the hoof (laminitis) and a form of eczema known as 'sweet itch'. The best grazing for a pony is found in what is called old pasture – that is, a field which has remained unploughed for several years, allowing a variety of grasses to become intermingled with other herbage, such as wild clover, dandelion, yarrow and vetches. These plants not only provide a varied diet but act as a guide to good land, since they will not grow on wet, acid soil, where stiff grasses give way to soft lush kinds that have little feeding value and may cause stomach upsets.

Fencing is the next problem. Barbed wire and any form of meshed fencing is dangerous for ponies: they may tear themselves on the first or get a foot entangled in the second. Posts and rails are the ideal kind of fencing and posts and plain

32

wire strands are the second choice, apart from hedges (of hawthorn or beech) or stone walls. Ponies vary in their capacity for getting out: some will stay placidly in the most sketchily fenced paddock, while others always believe that the grass is greener on the other side, and act accordingly; but it remains the duty of an owner to be sure that a pony is kept in, because a wandering one can damage crops and gardens or cause a traffic accident and thereby injure itself, too.

Since even a single pony on a couple of acres will produce a great deal of dung in a short time, part of the care of a paddock must involve collecting these droppings and removing them to a dung heap. This tiresome chore is essential to avoid more and more areas of the paddock becoming sour, and a build up of intestinal worm eggs, which are deposited in dung to survive among the grass stems and make the land what is known as 'horse sick' – a condition that makes the pasture unpalatable and the grazing animals liable to be infested by internal parasites.

There are several plants that are poisonous for ponies and so it is important to

Examples of good and bad fencing. The post-and-rail arrangement (*above, left*) is ideal, though expensive; barbed wire must *never* be used for any animal enclosure.

These plants and shrubs must be removed from the paddock or field where a pony is to be kept.

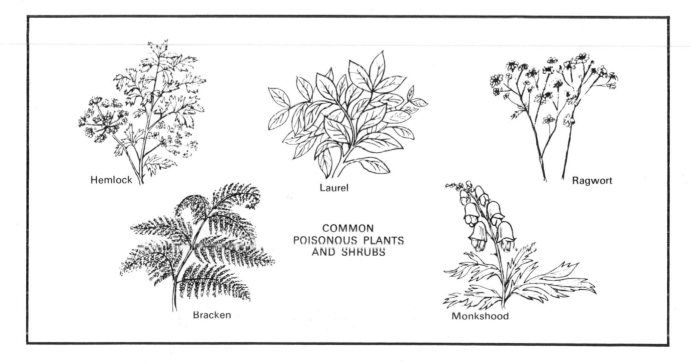

Hemlock

Laurel

Ragwort

Bracken

COMMON POISONOUS PLANTS AND SHRUBS

Monkshood

A strong post-and-rail fence at the right height for the size of the animal.

learn what these look like. Yew is perhaps the most dangerous; others include laburnum, laurel, rhododendron, privet and boxwood among the bushy types, while ragwort, monkshood (aconite), poison ivy, foxglove, nightshade, hellebore, meadow saffron (autumn crocus), hemlock, green bracken and henbane may be found along hedgerows or in the pasture. These are the sorts found in Britain. Other places will have other poisonous plants and all must be identified to be safe rather than sorry, and preferably grubbed up and burnt when they are found.

An ample supply of clean water in the paddock is essential. If there is a stream on one boundary the pony will not only drink there but enjoy paddling in hot weather, but it must be a clean stream, flowing and not stagnant, and not liable to pollution in its upper reaches (the absence or presence of fish is a guide to whether or not running water is polluted). However, a trough of some kind is a more usual means of supplying water. The best is the cattle type in which piped water is kept at a constant level by the action of a ballcock valve; a makeshift container, such as an old bath or cistern, can be kept topped up with the help of a garden hose. If a makeshift container is used, it must be carefully selected so that there are no sharp edges on which a pony could hurt itself. All water containers must be regularly cleaned, because ponies will go thirsty rather than drink dirty water. But, whatever kind is used, it must offer an unfailing supply, as a pony will drink several bucketfuls a day according to its size and needs.

Above: A well-built, durable and comfortable shelter in the paddock.

Below and right: Loose-boxes positioned to receive the maximum amount of light and sun. The stable doors have two bolts for safety and all electric cables and switches are fitted outside. The metal grille over the window is to prevent the pony from injuring itself on the glass.

35

In all seasons of the year, ponies benefit from a shelter in their paddock where they can escape from cold winds and driving rain or the torment of biting insects in hot weather. Field shelters are made by the manufacturers of timber stabling and consist of an open-fronted shed with a sloping or pent roof, which is sited to face away from the direction of the prevailing winds. In some, part of the front is also enclosed and in that case, when more than one pony is using the shelter, there should be two exits so that one animal cannot be cornered and bullied by another. Obviously, a handyman can make a cheaper form of shelter which will be adequate for the job, provided that it does not include any sharp edges, projecting nails or other sources of injury, and is weather and draught-proof.

The stable

Native ponies thrive best if they are kept out in a paddock with a shelter, but those with Arab or Thoroughbred blood need stabling at some times of the year; and, ideally, a stable is necessary to house a pony used for hunting, gymkhanas or showing, and while it is being groomed or handled in other ways, such as shoeing.

Years ago many stables consisted of stalls where horses were kept tied to a ring fixed by the manger, staring at a blank wall with nothing to occupy their minds except the next meal. Nowadays stables are generally made in the form of loose-boxes in which the animal is free to walk about, lie down to sleep, and look out over a half-door to take an interest in the passing scene.

Loose-boxes vary in size from 10ft (3m) square for a small pony to about 16ft (5m) for a large horse. The size needed for an individual pony is a matter for common sense, bearing in mind that it must have room to lie down at full stretch and be able to get up again without becoming 'cast' (see under Glossary and in the section on First Aid).

The doorway must be wide enough and high enough to avoid the chance of the animal knocking its body or head when entering or leaving.

While the top section of the half-door can be left open to admit light and air and allow the pony to look out, it is desirable to fit a window as well. This should be high in the front wall, because if all the air inlets are in one side there is no risk of a draught. Hinged at the bottom edge to fall inwards at an angle, it should be fixed by a latch that can vary the degree of opening. The reason for hinging in this manner is to funnel cold fresh air upwards towards the interior of the loose-box roof, where it will be slightly warmed before finding its way to a lower level. Windows must be protected inside with steel mesh or bars.

Nowadays floors are generally of concrete, marked with patterns to prevent hooves slipping. The most practical pattern is known as 'herring-bone' and is achieved by indenting the freshly-laid concrete with the edge of a plank to make a diagonal stripe running from the doorway to the opposite back corner, and then marking off several more lines at an angle to the main one as if you were drawing the flight end of an arrow. This not only provides a non-slip surface, but acts as a form of drain to take liquid, whether urine or an upset water bucket, towards the door.

Piped drains inside the stable are not satisfactory as they inevitably become choked, and fail altogether when peatmoss or sawdust is used as bedding; and, of course, stables have to be kept clean to maintain a pony's feet in a healthy state, which means that drainage should not be a problem. However, if you are building new loose-boxes and require plans to be approved by a local authority (as happens in Britain), it may be necessary to include a simple drainage system outside the stables before permission is granted.

Many people like to whitewash the interior of a stable on the principle that it looks nice and clean and, by reflection, increases the light. You can use an emulsion paint (*not* a paint containing poisonous lead) but this is expensive, while old-fashioned whitewash is cheaper and easily made. For an average loose-box you will need about 56lb (25kg) of unslaked or 'lump' lime, which a local builder can supply. Put this into an old bath or similar container and add the same amount of water by volume, more or less, so that it has the consistency of fairly thick soup. Some form of oil needs to be included in the mixture, linseed being the best but corn-oil will do, at the rate of two generous cupfuls to this amount of mix, well stirred in with a stick. Avoid any contact with the lime at this stage as it can burn your skin.

Leave the mixture in a safe place for about two days, while it bubbles and works to turn itself into a substance like white butter, when it is ready for use. Carve out enough of it to half-fill a bucket and then add more water to this, until it can be stirred into a thin paint ready to be applied to the walls. Wooden walls require a thicker whitewash mix than those built of brick or concrete blocks, which absorb a lot of the water. It is possible to buy brushes made for the purpose but, in fact, an old soft broom is a much better tool for the job, as you are less liable to become covered in whitewash yourself and, with a long handle, able to reach up the walls without using steps. Made-up whitewash no longer burns but it can sting your eyes, so avoid splattering it. The first coat will look very nice once it has dried, and if you renew it every six months or so the intensity of whiteness increases and keeps the stable walls clean and bright.

Stable fittings are optional, apart from a ring attached to one wall, which is essential for tying up a pony while it is groomed or otherwise handled. A manger may be used but the disadvantage here is that a pony in a loose box may dung into it, and even routine cleaning is difficult, so that feeding bowls are really preferable as these are removed between feeds. If your loose-box is fitted with a hay-rack it is better removed and replaced by a ring for tying a haynet, as a pony feeding from a rack tends to get seeds and dust falling into its eyes and this can lead to an eye infection.

A supply of fresh clean water is essential, because a thirsty pony will not eat or digest its food properly and, furthermore, when eventually offered water may

A well-equipped stable, with deep wheat-straw bedding, haynet and waterbucket firmly fixed to the wall.

drink too much at once, which is even less good for it. A supply piped to automatic bowls (originally designed for cattle) are good up to a point, but are rather difficult to keep clean. There are two types: one has a masked valve which refills the bowl as the water level goes down; the other has a flat lever in the base of the bowl which opens the valve when the drinking animal presses on it with its nose. In either type, the water makes a hissing noise when it is released. This may startle a pony not accustomed to an automatic drinker, so it may be necessary to supervise its first attempts to make certain that it understands and is able to use the bowl.

Since a pony will gladly employ its leisure in dismantling any fittings within reach, pipes leading to a fixed water bowl must be inset in the wall and the bowl clamped firmly. For the same reason, an electric light and its cable must be fixed in the roof and the switch sited outside.

Opinion conflicts about the use of mineral blocks in stables. Some owners maintain that a block fixed in a holder on the stable wall encourages a pony to the vice of crib-biting, while others believe firmly in the value of a permanent supply of minerals being available for the pony to lick according to its needs. Certainly, in areas where the soil (and therefore the water) is short of calcium, phosphates and salts, additional minerals are needed and most ponies will come to no harm by obtaining them from a block.

Bedding

Bedding in a stable serves two purposes. It provides comfort, which encourages a pony to rest and sleep lying down, and is also an absorbent base to soak up dung and water. Wheat straw and peatmoss are the best kinds of bedding or litter, with a mixture of sawdust and woodshavings as an alternative. Barley straw is bad because it carries prickles that can irritate an animal's skin; and oat straw lacks elasticity, is not very absorbent, but is palatable, which may lead a pony to eat its bed – an unhealthy habit that may be difficult to break.

Wheat straw is supplied in bales of varying size, averaging about 40lb (18kg) in weight which gives you, say, sixty bales to a ton (1,000kg). It should be stored in a dry place, preferably on a layer of brushwood if the floor is earthen or concrete to prevent the bottom layer from becoming damp and musty. Musty straw or hay is very bad for animals and humans alike, as dust particles from it can cause lung infection.

Peatmoss also comes in bales. One type is meant for use in the garden and is of a finer grade, usually sold damp and compressed into a block; this is worse than useless for the stable where a dry thick bed is required, so be sure that you buy the right sort and store it carefully.

Sawdust alone is too dusty for stable use but is improved when mixed with shavings or thin chippings. The drawback to it is that once wet it clogs and soon becomes damp and uncomfortable as bedding. A proportion of about one-third sawdust to two-thirds peatmoss will save on some peat, which is comparatively expensive, and give a reasonably satisfactory bed.

Mucking-out

This is the first morning chore after watering and feeding has been completed. A straw bed should be sorted out with a fork, moving dung and dirty straw to the door and tossing the remaining clean material into a corner so that the floor can be swept with a stiff broom. If the pony is out during the day, then leave the bare floor to dry, but otherwise replace the bed, well shaken up, and add new bedding as necessary. The first thing most ponies do with a clean bed is to stale on it, which immediately undoes part of your hard work in preparing a nice dry floor. For this reason it is worth sacrificing a little clean straw out in the yard and taking the pony to that before returning it to the stable.

Peat bedding, on the other hand, is left where it is while you collect dung with a short-handled shovel and a bucket, and put aside any soaked patches of peat into a separate bucket (as this may be suitable for re-use after drying in the sun). The clean peat is then raked vigorously to regain its spring and make the stable tidy. Sawdust and shavings receive the same treatment.

It is worth establishing a separate area to store stable manure, because if it is merely thrown into a heap it will become more and more unsightly as weather

Mucking out the stable is an essential part of the daily routine.

acts upon it, spreading out the base. The simplest means of keeping the heap tidy is to drive four posts into the ground and fix sheets of corrugated iron lengthwise to enclose three sides of the square, with the open side facing your route with a loaded barrow. If the posts and iron are treated with a bituminous paint, both will last longer.

Foods and feeding

Hay is the basic food for ponies not at grass and during the winter. Its value lies in the fact that it is not dry in the same way as, for example, dead leaves, but is cured in the sun so that it retains the goodness of the grass from which it was made. Well-made hay derived from nutritious grass is an excellent food, but, equally, well-made hay from a field of weeds lacks nutrition and so does the best grass when it is badly cured.

There are three main types of hay produced in Britain: seed hay, which is made from a field sown with selected grasses; clover hay, made from red clover with, usually, some ryegrass included; and meadow hay, made from a mixture of grasses in an established field. It is not difficult to detect bad hay – it has a dirty look and an unpleasant peppery smell; rubbishy hay has a lot of soft grass in it, with perhaps one or two large leaves which may have been docks, and lacks any smell. Good hay is still slightly green in colour and has a pleasant sweetish smell,

The essential supplementary nutrients of your pony's diet if you expect him to do a lot of work.

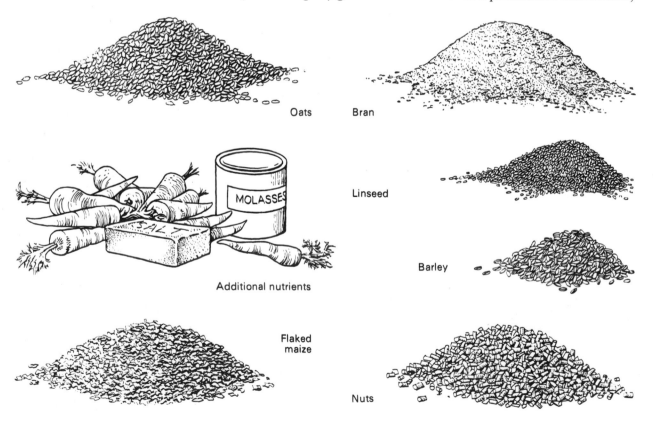

Oats

Bran

Linseed

Barley

Additional nutrients

Flaked maize

Nuts

The feed room. Notice the large metal containers which keep the food dry and free from vermin.

while the grasses in it have fairly stiff stalks. To judge a sample bale, first sniff it and then thump an end on the ground – if it bounces in your hands it is good.

Alfalfa, or lucerne, seldom thrives in Britain, which is unfortunate as it is the best of all fodder for the horse family, widely used in the United States and other countries where the climate is suitable. In recent years, the haulm (green tops) of the ground-nut have been made into hay with some success in parts of Australia.

If you have a spare patch in the vegetable garden, it is possible to produce a valuable crop of green food for one or two ponies by sowing a few rows of sweet corn (maize) in the spring. It will be ready to cut as required from August until the end of September; ponies love to eat it raw and thrive on it, just at a time when

41

grazing is becoming poor and it is too early to start feeding hay. Sweet corn does best in rich soil and what better use could be made of stable manure!

Fresh foods are valuable in winter to augment hay and cereals. Carrots are much enjoyed and so are apples; some ponies will eat mangolds, others refuse to touch them. When feeding root vegetables, be sure to wash them clean of earth and check that they are not frosted, as this can cause internal upsets. All these foods should be roughly cut up into bite-sized pieces to avoid the possibility of the pony choking.

Cereals or the 'short feed' for ponies in normal work should not include oats, as this highly energizing food can make them unmanageable, but up to 2lb (1kg) may be given after a day's hunting or other strenuous activity. Cubed feeds ('pony nuts') are now made for ponies and this is a very satisfactory method of feeding, providing a balanced diet with little or no waste. The only problem then is one of monotony, but this can be avoided by adding to the ration a handful of flaked maize or the same of broad bran, with a few sliced carrots or chopped apple. Dried sugar-beet pulp is available in some places and can be fed in moderation after being soaked in water overnight — never feed it dry because it swells and could cause severe colic. Lastly, the nice treacly taste of molasses may be added; this is too sticky to be fed alone but is obtainable as molassine meal and is an excellent food. Titbits, in the form of bread and sugar, should, of course, be avoided.

A food store is an obvious requirement. This is often combined with the tack room but that is a mistake, unless lack of space makes it unavoidable, because saddlery which has been put up with a covering of oil while not in immediate use will be found to have added a coating of dust when it is taken down. Ideally, the food store should be near the stables and, besides containing bins of food, have a bale of hay handy for refilling haynets for the night. Bins of some kind are essential, as sacks of food attract vermin and do not keep well once opened; cornbins with a flap lid are best, but plastic dustbins of the larger sort serve the purpose just as well, where reasonably small amounts of stocks are kept.

Assuming that you buy hay and straw in bulk, which is most economical, this should be stored well away from the stables because of the fire risk.

The equipment needed to feed one or two ponies includes a feed scoop for measuring out rations; feeding bowls of galvanized iron with a flat base; water buckets – which should be of the pliable plastic type (hard plastic cracks if trodden on by a pony) and of a different colour to those used for collecting dung; and several haynets.

Handling ponies

The guiding principle in handling ponies is to let the animal know where you are and what you are going to do. So, on arriving at the door of its box, you should speak to the pony before entering and if it is by the door tell it, firmly, to 'stand

To pick up the pony's foot, run your hand down its leg, leaning against its shoulder to make it transfer the weight on to the other legs; as your hand reaches the fetlock, pull up the foot and cradle it in your hand.

over' – move out of your way. Never shove past a pony because this invites it to start a shoving match. Stable manners are very important and must be impressed upon a pony from the first, so that it will stand still, stand over, and show no resistance when its feet are picked up – in the last instance the command 'foot' is as good as any.

Any approach should begin with a hand on the animal, placed firmly since a gentle touch can suggest a fly. If, for example, you propose to fit a halter, pat its neck and then buckle on the halter, chatting as you do so; or to pick up a front leg, put your hand on the withers and work it smoothly down towards the knee, saying 'foot'. The pony will soon learn to lift a foot if this command is always given. Unfailing kindness coupled with a no-nonsense attitude will teach a pony to submit willingly, as its feelings of affection, trust and respect grow. This must be the basis of your relationship if you are to become successful partners.

43

On the other side of the coin is the owner who is rough and cross, gives orders in a tone that clearly expects disobedience and, having got what he expected from a flustered pony, fails to insist on discipline. His pony behaves badly out of bewilderment, resenting this treatment and responding by any means at its disposal.

Grooming

The obvious reason for grooming a pony is in order to keep its coat, mane and tail free of dirt, loose hairs and scurf, but there is another, equally important, purpose and that is as a form of massage.

A grooming kit consists of the following: a *hoof pick*, a blunt iron hook used to remove accumulated dirt from the feet; a *dandy brush*, which is stiff for use on hard-caked dirt; a *body brush* and *curry comb*, always used together – the brush for grooming and the curry comb for keeping the brush clean as you work; a *water brush*, which has soft bristles, is used to damp the mane and tail, for washing the legs if this is necessary, and also for grooming the head and face where a harder brush is too harsh for sensitive skin. Add to these *two sponges*, one for cleaning eyes and nostrils and the other for the dock; a *metal comb* for the mane and tail; *stable rubbers*, which may be cotton teatowels or squares torn from an old sheet, and are used for a final polish on a groomed coat; and a *sweat-scraper*, which is designed to remove lathered sweat but, as your pony should not be allowed to get into this undesirable state, can be usefully employed in the course of drying a rain-soaked animal.

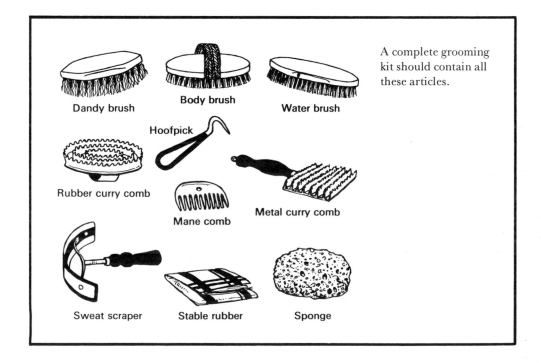

Dandy brush

Body brush

Water brush

Hoofpick

Rubber curry comb

Mane comb

Metal curry comb

Sweat scraper

Stable rubber

Sponge

A complete grooming kit should contain all these articles.

In summer all ponies should be groomed, to a greater or lesser extent depending on whether or not they are entered for shows. Winter grooming, however, should be very restricted if an animal is living out, as a thorough brushing would remove the natural weather-proofing effect of the oil in its coat. It should receive only brief attention just to clear any caked mud on its body and legs, and keep the mane and tail free of tangles. But riding ponies which are stabled at night and in bad weather, or are wholly or partially clipped, must be groomed properly, winter and summer, as a matter of routine.

The principles of grooming have been handed down over the course of centuries by way of cavalry regiments and the stables of hunting squires to arrive at a method which has become the standard way to groom a horse or pony.

Tie up the pony to a ring on the stable wall, and then start by picking out its feet with a hoof pick, using it carefully round the sensitive sole and frog. At the same time, check the shoes and the 'clenches' – the nails holding the shoe in place. Assuming that there is no dirt to be removed by a dandy brush, take the body brush in your left hand and the curry comb in your right, stand away from the pony on the nearside (that is, the left side) so that you must lean slightly forwards to reach it, and start work on the neck behind its ear, using a semi-circular motion in the same direction as the hair grows. The brush should be drawn across the curry comb at intervals to clear the bristles of dust and hair.

Work down to the shoulder, the chest and between the forelegs, and then on down the near foreleg to the coronet, paying careful attention to the heel. Change hands, brushing with the right, to work under the body; change back again to go on with the back, side, flank and quarters; completing that side of the animal by working down the near hind leg. To groom the off side work as before, but reversing the brush and curry comb to right and left hands.

Brush the pony's face gently, and then, taking up the body brush or dandy brush (best to use if the mane is very thick), do its mane and tail (the metal comb is used only for tangles as it is liable to tear the hairs). The sponges, slightly damped, should be used to wipe round the eyes, nostrils and dock in that order. Lastly, complete the job by going over the entire animal with a clean stable rubber to give a final polish and prove to yourself that the job has been done properly – if it has, the rubber will remain clean.

Most manes lie on the off side of the neck but if one is left ungroomed it may become untidy, when it can usually be persuaded back with the help of a damp water brush. Some ponies have very thick manes which can be intractable; they will need to be 'pulled' (see page 113) before they will lie neatly over to one side. Hooves look better for a wipe over with oil, which also benefits the horn, particularly in a hoof that is inclined to brittleness. Dark hooves can be treated with hoof oil and light ones with neatsfoot.

The first few days of grooming regularly will prove very tiring but have the advantage of involving exercise that will help to get you fit for riding. As to the need for all this hard work, it is essential in order to keep a pony in good

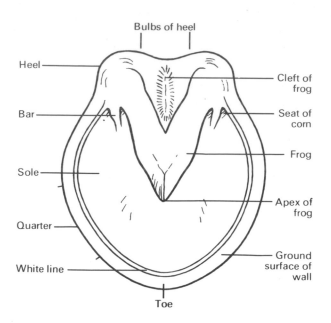

How to tie a quick-release knot.

Right: A diagram of the underside of the foot, showing the fleshy frog.

Bulbs of heel

Heel

Bar

Sole

Quarter

White line

Toe

Cleft of frog

Seat of corn

Frog

Apex of frog

Ground surface of wall

Above: Removing dirt from the foot with a hoof pick; always work towards the toe.

Right: Here you can see the 'clenches' (nails) which hold the shoe on to the foot. It does not hurt to have the clenches hammered in, because this part of the foot is not sensitive.

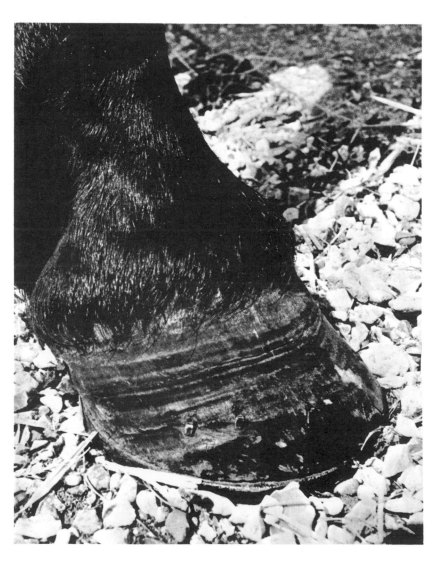

46

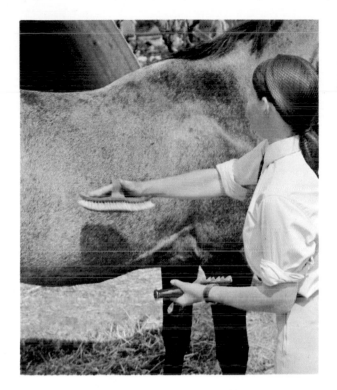

Above left, and left: Use a body brush as part of the daily grooming routine, cleaning it after every few strokes on a metal or rubber curry comb.

Above: The body brush is also used to brush out the pony's tail.

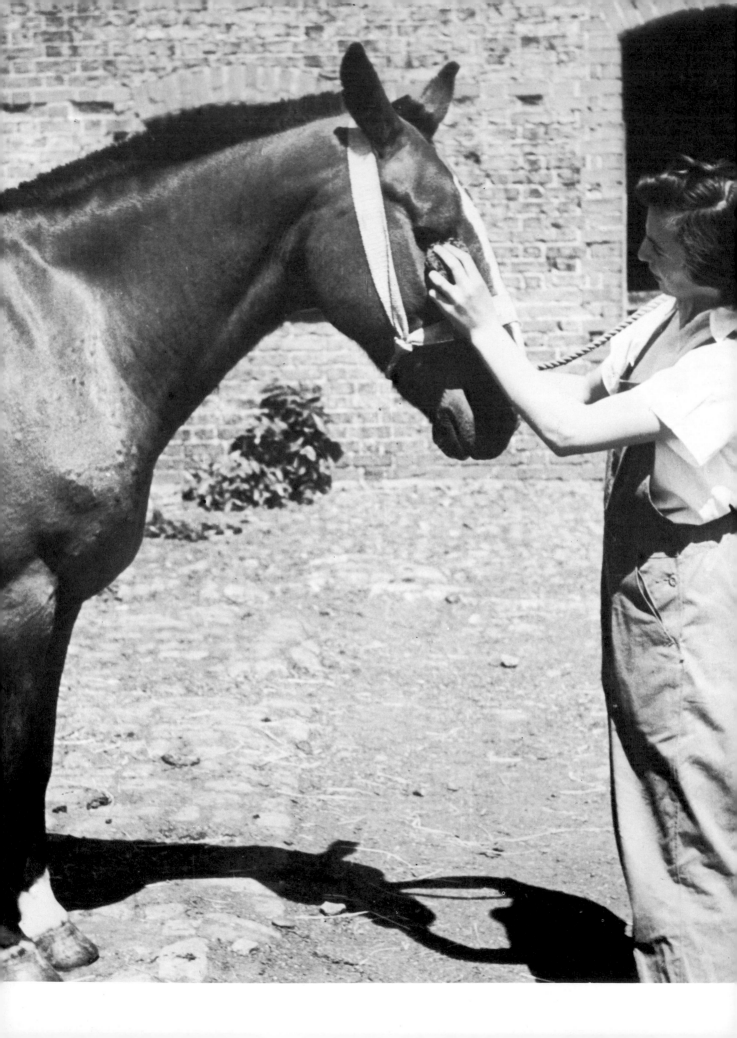

condition, and you will find that it becomes easier and, eventually, automatic as time goes by.

So far, the grooming has been what could be described as cosmetic—cleaning and polishing the coat and, to some extent, toning the muscles. Real massage grooming for the purpose of building muscle and getting the pony into hard condition is known as wisping or banging. A wisp is always home-made and consists of a rope of twisted hay with two loops at one end, through which the rope is plaited alternately to achieve a reasonably neat bundle. You can learn to make one quite easily (see the diagram on this page).

Wisping is an art and what you are aiming at is thumping the pony's muscles so that they react by tightening in anticipation of the next bang, and so get stronger and larger, while the skin responds by secreting oil which adds a gloss to the coat. Begin this work fairly mildly on a pony that is not accustomed to wisping and gradually build up the action until you are hitting reasonably hard with a wisp bundle, using the whole arm and the weight of your body. Common sense will tell you *not* to bang the loins (which would hurt the pony) or any bony parts of its body; the object is the development of muscles in the neck, shoulders and quarters, and this will be achieved in a surprisingly short time by wisping for about twenty minutes in the morning and evening. Of course, exercise and careful feeding also play an important part in this process.

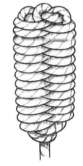

How the wisp is twisted into shape.

While plaiting manes and pulling tails is generally considered as part of grooming, this subject is dealt with in the section on riding in competitions (see pages 113-16), since it is virtually obligatory at shows.

Stable routine

All animals, and ponies in particular, benefit under management founded on routine. This can be a problem when spare-time is limited, and it is difficult to lay down absolute rules to fit individual circumstances, but there is a framework of facts to be considered: a stabled pony needs a clean loose-box, regular grooming, exercise, and several small feeds in the course of a day. Without these four essentials it will not thrive. Even a pony out at grass needs daily attention—a check and a chat at the very least.

Beginning with summer management and taking as an average size a pony of 13.2 hands, it will be at grass when not working—that is, training for or taking part in shows and gymkhanas. This animal will need about 1lb (500g) of cubes when it is brought in at breakfast time, and a second feed at, say, four pm of 4lb (2kg) cubes and 1lb (500g) bran. If it is away from home during the day then it should have hay and some cut greenfood when not active.

A pony that is doing no work at all, perhaps while its owner is away at school, can be left on grass alone provided that the grazing is good, but, of course, it will have to be brought back into condition before it can be expected to work again.

In the winter a pony living out at grass, with a field shelter and doing no work,

49

Here the groom is using one of the sponges gently to clean round the eyes and nostrils.

needs a morning feed of 4lb (2kg) hay and 3lb (1.5kg) cubes, with 5lb (2.2kg) hay, and some sliced carrots, as an evening feed. This will maintain the pony until it is required to work, when a period of up to three weeks will be necessary to get it into condition for hunting or similar activity.

The same pony stabled, clipped and working, will need at least four feeds a day, which should be divided as follows:
8 am: 2lb (1kg) cubes, 2lb (1kg) hay; *midday:* 3lb (1.5kg) cubes, 2lb (1kg) hay; *4 pm:* cereal mixture—cubes, bran, flaked maize (and oats if hard worked)—totalling 4lb (2kg) with sliced carrots added, and 5lb (2.2kg) hay. *8 pm:* a final check before bedtime may show that a little more hay is required to occupy the pony through the night.

Once a routine of feeding is established it must be regular, because ponies are very aware of time and become upset if their food fails to appear at the correct hour. A second important point is that the animal must be given time to eat and digest its meals, and this means about twenty minutes eating time for a cereal feed and one and a half hours in which to digest it. So, on a hunting day for example when you are allowing an hour to hack to a meet arranged for eleven am, you will start grooming and saddling-up at nine o'clock, and the pony must have been fed two hours earlier at seven. In this case, the routine *is* altered by an hour but does not matter; it is delay in feeding which causes frustration.

Feeding a pony correctly according to its needs requires common sense and experience. Clearly, you would not bring a pony in from grass and start it on a full working diet of cereals; changes in foods must be gradual to avoid upsetting the animal's stomach, and increased by degrees as it gains condition by means of exercise and grooming. The time allowed for digestion is important, because the stomach lies next to the chest and work on a full stomach can, therefore, affect the pony's breathing and put a strain on its heart.

Equally, ponies vary in the amount of food they need, and so there can be no hard and fast rules laid down for the total daily intake—what may be right for one pony may be too much or too little for another—but the amounts listed can be taken as a rough guide. The point to remember is that a pony has a small stomach, designed to contain a little food most of the time and not a lot of food every now and again.

While feeding is the most important factor in stable management, cleanliness is vital, too. A loose-box must be mucked out every day, and droppings removed whenever possible during the day to keep the floor and bedding clean. A stabled pony must have exercise and it must be groomed, and all this combines to make keeping a pony in good condition a lot of hard work for its owner.

Exercise

Exercise for a pony serves the same purpose as training for an athlete. An animal brought in from grass is, or should be, very healthy with a nice gloss on its

Above: Hacking along country lanes is pleasant exercise for both pony and rider.

Left: Hill work is an excellent method of developing muscles and improving balance.

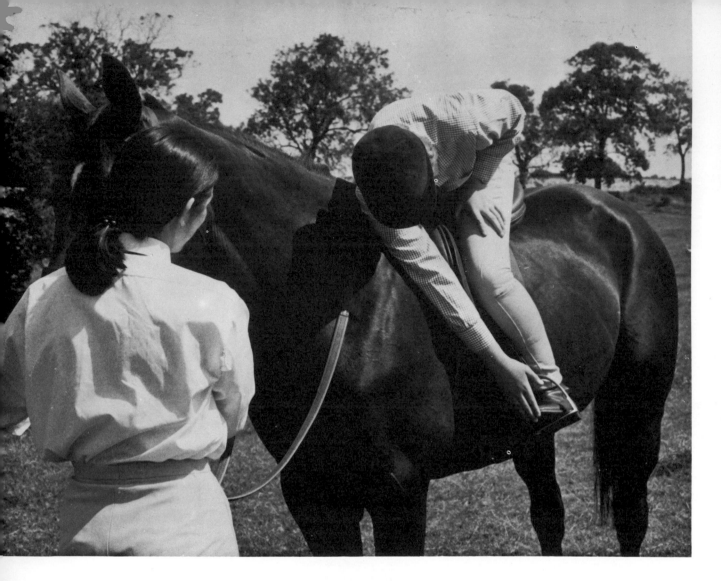

A good balancing and suppling exercise is to bend over and touch your toes while sitting in the saddle.

summer coat, but its muscles are slack. The object of exercise is to remove excess fat and to harden and enlarge the muscles so that the pony feels strong and full of energy.

The first stage should consist of walking, on the flat for the first few days and then up and down hills. Walking up hill develops the quarters, loins and forearms; while walking down hill brings the hocks under and helps to achieve balance.

Trotting is the next phase, alternating with walking, until the pony is trotting up hill without undue effort. Cantering and galloping, strangely enough, have little bearing on muscle development and fitness and, in fact, can do harm in the early stages of conditioning. Common sense will set a time limit to the exercise period, which will vary according to the pony's condition. It takes from six to eight weeks to bring a pony into condition from grass, and the daily exercise should be built up from half an hour to a maximum of two hours over this period of time.

When the pony is back in working shape, having lost its 'grass-belly' and begun to muscle-up, it can begin canters, gallops, school work and jumping for a

52

sensible amount of time until it is truly fit for shows or hunting. By this time it must have daily exercise without fail. But always remember not to overtire or bore your pony by too long and monotonous a working session.

Fitness applies to the rider as well, who may need exercises, too. Some can be done in the saddle, rising and slowly resuming the seat while at the walk; turning round to look back on either side, and trotting without stirrups. On the ground you can practise arm-swinging and touching your toes. The muscle on the inside of the thighs can be very uncomfortable at first, but pulling the muscle on each leg back so that it lies against the saddle will prove helpful until strength is gained.

A trace clip is the most suitable kind of clip for most ponies, but do not attempt to clip your pony yourself until you have learned from an expert.

Clipping

Ponies begin to look rough as the winter coat starts to grow at the end of the summer. The coat varies in thickness according to the breed; mountain and moorland ponies naturally have a very thick one as a protection against harsh weather; a pony with Arab or Thoroughbred ancestry may show little change.

53

The objects of clipping are to enable an animal to work hard and fast without losing condition by heavy sweating, and to reduce the problem of drying a rain-soaked coat and the work involved in grooming. There are several types of clip: a *full clip* removes the whole coat; a *hunter clip* leaves the legs and a saddle-patch; a *blanket clip*, in which only the neck and belly are clipped; and the *trace clip*, which corresponds with the line of a harness trace, under the belly and down the legs to include half of the forearm and thigh.

Clipping is an art and it is wise to employ a professional to do the job for you. The pony must be dry and thoroughly groomed, and you will need a rug to cover the clipped animal—which may be kept occupied with a haynet during the operation. As to the type of clip to choose, you should take advice on this according to the work that the pony has to do. On the whole, a trace clip is perhaps the most suitable.

Shoeing

A good blacksmith, or farrier, is vital to the proper care of ponies. While at grass the shoes are removed, but feet still require regular attention so that they are kept level and in good shape. A working pony needs a set of shoes, correctly fitted and nailed, with a life dependent on the amount of hard roadwork done, but always taken off and replaced (or renewed) every month so that the hoof remains level and does not outgrow its shoe. The method of shoeing may be either hot or cold. Hot shoeing is the traditional way and still the best, but usually involves taking the pony to a blacksmith's forge, whereas travelling smiths can fit cold shoes in your own yard. The point to remember is that a shoe must fit the hoof and not the other way round.

First aid

Saving on vet's bills is a false economy, but it may be necessary to take some action while waiting for him to arrive, and so it is essential to have a first-aid cupboard or box in the tack room in case of accidents or sudden illness.

The medicine chest should contain bandages of various sizes including the crêpe (elasticated) type packets of cotton wool; a large pack of 'Animalintex', which combines lint and wool for animal treatment; a puffer of antibiotic powder; and some form of medication for an attack of colic, preferably an injection if you can safely learn how to administer it (see page 56).

Cast This is not a common occurrence but seems more prevalent in part-Arab and part-Thoroughbred ponies. What happens is that the animal lies down in its box and possibly rolls, getting itself into a position where it is unable to regain its legs—lying half on its back with the feet against a side wall. If the pony then panics, it can damage its legs, or choke on sicked-up water or food. Should you come across this situation there are two points to remember: !rst of all, keep calm

The blacksmith at work. Here he is 'hot shoeing', fitting the shoe exactly to the foot.

yourself and talk reassuringly to the pony, and, second, avoid getting kicked while turning it over. Turning needs two people with a halter and a rope, and two separate lengths of rope knotted at one end to form nooses. The halter is put on the pony's head and the two nooses slipped over the *underside* fore and hind legs, when all three ropes are pulled at the same time to turn the head, neck and body together. As the pony turns over, let go and stand clear, allowing room for it to scramble to its feet; then make a soothing fuss of it, check for cuts and bruises, and move the animal to a larger loose-box.

Colic As a rule, colic is due to mismanagement such as a sudden change in diet, or because the animal is infested with worms. The symptoms are obvious: the pony sweats, paws the ground, turns its head towards a flank, attempts to kick its belly, and may roll—all in an effort to remove a severe stomach ache. First of all, call the veterinary surgeon, making it clear that this is an emergency, and then keep the pony on its feet. A rug, and warm cloths applied to the stomach region, may be helpful, and if you have a hypodermic syringe containing a dose for colic in your medicine chest, use this promptly. Many people find it hard to bring

55

themselves to give an injection, but it is very useful if you can learn how to do it correctly. Your vet will show you, but, basically, it involves thumping the site (usually the neck) with your fist three or four times and then using the needle on the final thump, which is scarcely felt by the animal; you then attach the body of the hypodermic to the needle and gently press the plunger home.

Lameness The causes of lameness are legion, but common sense will tell you to check first that the pony has not got a stone wedged in the sole of its foot, which even when removed may leave a bruise and consequent lameness for a day or two. If that is not the reason, you must call professional advice.

Wounds These may involve cuts of varying kinds and puncture wounds. Minor cuts should be washed with plain water and dusted with antibiotic powder. Larger injuries accompanied by bleeding may need stitching by a vet and he should be called; meanwhile, it is urgent to stop the flow of blood and this can be done by applying pressure above and below the wound if it is on a limb, or by pinching it with your fingers if the site is in a place where it is impossible to fix a tight bandage effectively. Remember to loosen a tight bandage at intervals of about four minutes, because if the normal blood supply is cut off from a limb for any length of time this can result in permanent damage. Ice cubes, wrapped in a clean cloth and applied to a bleeding wound, will often stem the flow by causing a clot to form. If you bandage a wound before the vet arrives, clean it first with water but leave other treatment to him. Antiseptics should not be used with antibiotic powder, as one will prevent the other from doing any good. Puncture wounds, perhaps due to a splinter or to barbed wire, sometimes appear minor but must be taken seriously, because dirt and microbes may have been 'injected', and if left untreated can result in inflammation under the surface of the healing skin and even an abscess.

Finally, there is the problem of tetanus. Most sensible people have their ponies inoculated against this as foals, but it is just as important to keep up with booster injections at intervals according to the veterinary surgeon's advice, because the smallest prick from a blackthorn bush or any minor wound can admit germs.

Buying a pony

When the exciting time arrives for you to own a pony, actually buying the right animal is very important and there are so many factors to be taken into account. Assuming that you have learned the elements of riding at a riding school, the size of pony that suited you there should give a guide to the size to buy, but it must be borne in mind that a small pony may be sadly out-grown all too soon. Equally, if your main interest is in hunting and Pony Club activities, a fine show pony may not meet your needs. All this ought to be considered before you begin to look for a pony of your own.

56

This pony looks kind and reliable. Its eyes are friendly with no white showing; its ears are pricked forward indicating alertness; it has an intelligent expression.

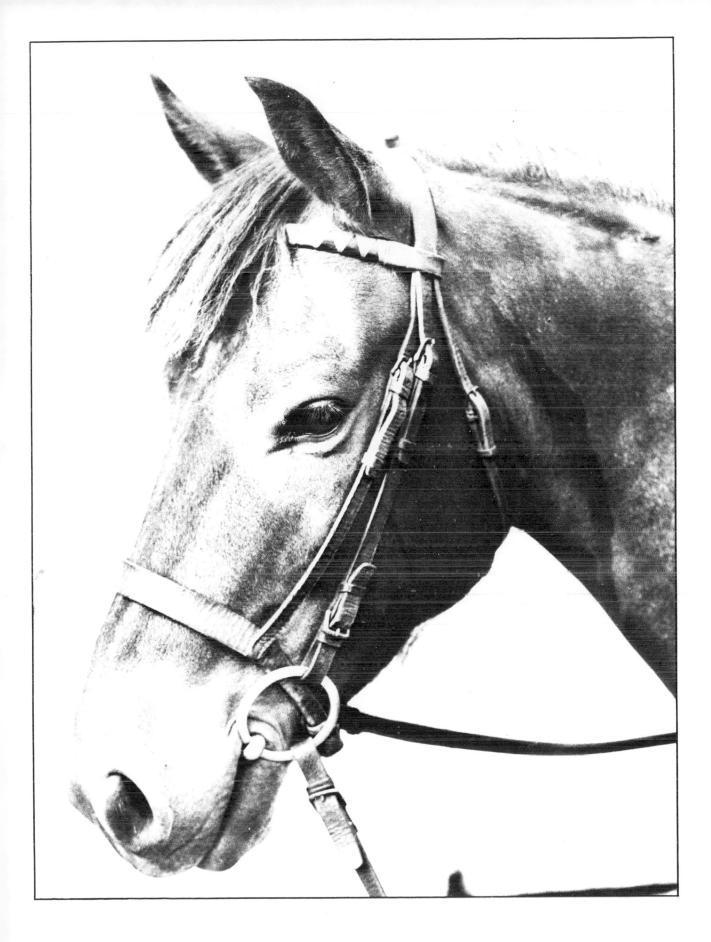

These two ponies are both ideal first ponies; kind and quiet and good to learn on.

There are various ways of setting out to buy a pony, but one of the best chances of success is with an animal that has been out-grown by a friend (or the friend of a friend), as it is unlikely to have serious faults or they would not have kept it in the first place. The next alternative is by way of an advertisement in a local newspaper or in a horse magazine; and, lastly, there are auction sales held in many country districts, where a wide variety of horses and ponies are offered.

A wise novice will avoid auctions like the plague because, while good ponies are sometimes sold in them and it is even possible to find a wonderful bargain, a large number are entered for some undesirable reason (carefully masked on the day), such as chronic bad feet or a wilful temperament. In this case it would be wise to take an expert with you, who can give professional advice.

58

This leaves friends and advertisements. In either case, great care should be exercised before making a final choice, as this can mean the difference between the enjoyment of owning and riding a pony, and the depressing realization that you have made an expensive mistake.

When you plan to look at a particular pony take a knowledgeable person with you, who will not only be able to give an opinion about its worth, but can watch you ride it and see whether or not you suit each other. As a first step, you should ask the owner to walk the pony away and then back, and then repeat the process at a trot—leading it so that you can note if it runs crab-wise instead of straight or shows even the smallest sign of lameness. Then see it ridden, again straight back and forth at the walk and trot, and circling at a canter, and, lastly, taking one or

59

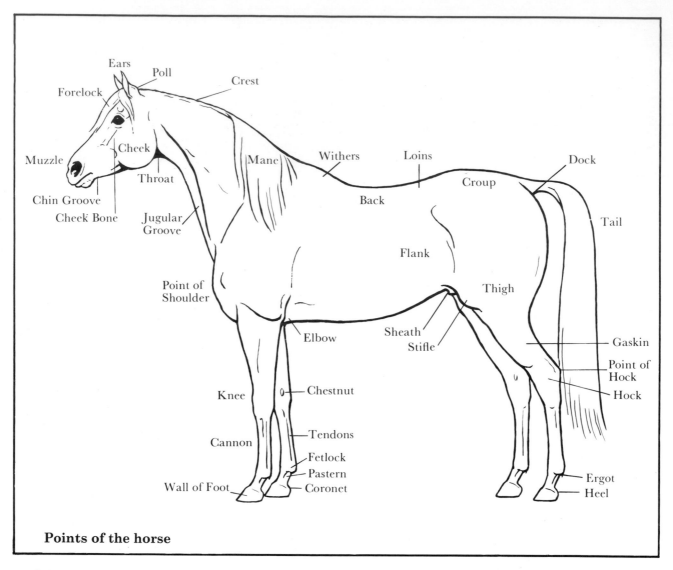

Points of the horse

Being able to identify the points of your pony will help you to look after it better.

two jumps. This should give a clear idea of its soundness, and it is time for you to ride the pony yourself.

Before mounting, chat to the pony. It should have a kind, bold eye with the shine of health, and respond to petting without attempting to nip, shy away or show the white of its eye. When you mount, make sure that it stands still until you ask for a move and then apply the aids gently. There now remains the all-important point, is this pony going to be your friend and measure up to the vision you have had of your first pony? If so, then arrange for a veterinary inspection as a final check before the purchase is completed. Many genuine owners will allow you to have a pony on trial for a few days before the sale is finalized.

When the pony arrives at its new home with you, remember that this is an upsetting experience for it. You are a stranger and its surroundings are unknown,

60

so give it time to settle down. On your first ride keep to a walk, talking to the animal in a soothing voice, but be firm in insisting on obedience; then turn it out to find its way about the paddock and take some exercise, before stabling it for the night. Never leave a new arrival out at night until it has become accustomed to its new home, because it may break out and injure itself or become lost. As the days go by ask a little more of the pony until you can canter and jump without any doubt about the outcome, but always go back to the previous stage and get that right if the pony fails to answer your directions. Be patient, because the fault may be yours, but remain firmly in charge so that you do not lose its respect.

4 Tack

Tack, which is the general name for all kinds of saddlery, can prove very expensive if it is bought new, but most saddlers have a stock of second-hand items at reasonable prices. Leather will last for a long time if it is treated properly and kept supple with saddle-soap and a certain amount of 'elbow grease'. Equally, neglected leather dries, cracks and finally breaks, which makes old tack possibly dangerous in use. So inspect carefully before buying it, paying attention to its feel in your hands and checking that the stitching is in good order. The basic outfit for a pony is a bridle, a bit, and a saddle with stirrups and a girth.

Bridles and bits

In simple terms, the object of a bridle is to hold the bit in a pony's mouth by means of a strap, which passes up the side of its face, behind the ears and down to be attached to the bit on the opposite side. This strap is called the cheek-piece and is kept in place in front of the ears by the brow band and by the throat-lash, which runs under the upper part of the jaw where it joins the neck. Most bridles also include a noseband held by a secondary cheek-piece; this is usually there only to look smart, except when it is used with a standing martingale. This describes a normal snaffle bridle suitable for most ponies.

A saddler will know the correct size of bridle if he is told the height of the pony and its breed. This last point is important, since Welsh and part-Arab ponies tend to have rather smaller heads in relation to their height.

To put on a bridle work from the near side. Hold the head piece in your right hand and the bit between the forefinger and thumb of your left hand, which should then slide under the pony's chin, allowing the remaining three fingers to feel between its lips where there is a gap between the teeth. The pony will then open its mouth and accept the bit while the bridle is drawn up and, with the left hand now free, the head piece placed behind each ear in turn. Now do up the buckles, working down the face in order, allowing a full hand's breadth between the throat-lash and the cheek and the space of two fingers under the noseband. After checking that the bridle is level with no part twisted and that the mane and forelock are smoothed down, then finish the buckling by putting each strap end

A well-fitting eggbutt snaffle with carefully adjusted noseband – a good combination for a child's pony.

into its 'keeper' and 'runner' (a keeper is an attached loop and a runner is a sliding loop).

Bits are made in a variety of patterns but only two types need concern the pony owner. These are the jointed and straight-bar snaffles and the Pelham. But before discussing the fitting and use of a bit it is as well to understand how it works in a pony's mouth. Our own teeth are normally set one beside the other in a half moon, whereas the jaw of the horse family is shaped like a long narrow U with the front teeth (the incisors) divided from the back teeth (the molars) by gaps of gum on each side, called the 'bars'. These bars are level with the corner of the mouth and consist of a fine membrane laced with nerves covering the jaw bone.

A bit lies across the tongue and over the bars to join the reins on either side of the mouth. A jointed- or plain-snaffle bit, properly used, acts on the outside of the bars, on the lips or on the corners of the mouth depending on the hands that hold the reins, while the Pelham also exerts some pressure on the tongue and surface of the bars. Clearly, good hands are essential for a good rider on a responsive pony, because rough use of the reins will have two effects: to start with, the pony will pull in a vain effort to get away from the rider who it knows is causing the pain in its mouth; and then, after a time, nerves in the bars will be destroyed and the pony will have a numb or 'hard' mouth.

The snaffle is simple to fit. It should be wide enough to lie comfortably across the pony's mouth and be joined to the cheek-pieces of the bridle without wrinkling the corners of the lips. Make sure that it is level by using the same hole number on each buckle of the bridle. Jointed snaffles are metal, but a plain, straight-bar snaffle can be made of rubber, vulcanite or metal. A non-metal bit is comparatively gentle, provided that the pony is not inclined to a dry mouth, when it can stick to the mouth and cause sore lips.

The Pelham bit is slightly more complicated than a snaffle as it has three rings on each end of the mouthpiece to carry two reins: the upper ring is attached to the cheek-piece, the second to what is called the snaffle rein and the third to the lower or curb rein. Furthermore, there is a curb chain and lip strap to fit.

A curb chain is made to lie flat in the groove of the chin, looped on to hooks fixed to the upper bit rings. This is achieved by attaching one end to the offside hook and then, working from the near side, twisting the chain until it is flat with the central loose ring hanging down. The chain will be two or three links too long and so the last link is hooked and then the spares taken up and hooked so as to leave room for a thumb flat between the chain and the pony's jaw. This device acts with the bit to exert pressure on the bars of the mouth, with the effect that the head is lowered and brought in towards the pony's chest, giving greater flexion.

The lip strap on a Pelham has two purposes: to prevent the chain coming undone and the pony from taking hold of the cheeks of the bit. It is attached to a D ring fixed just above the lower bit rings, passing through the centre ring of the curb chain.

While types of bit and their variations are legion, the two basic kinds have opposite effects. The snaffle type tends to raise the pony's head; while the Pelham lowers it and, by means of the curb rein, brings the chin towards the chest, which can cause great discomfort to a pony with a short thick neck, as it is unable to flex correctly and so tries to escape by pulling.

As a general principle it can be said that a pony is less likely to fight a plain bit (e.g., a straight-bar snaffle). It must be remembered that the stronger the pull on the reins the more the pony will try to exert its own will, and that is why a light hand is so important, conveying firmly but gently messages that the animal can understand and obey. Very severe bits, such as long-cheeked double bridles and gag snaffles, will certainly control a pony, but this is not the good rider's way, and, as a general rule, the simpler the bit is the better.

Snaffles

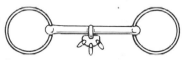

Breaking bit with keys

Loose ring mullen mouth
snaffle

Loose ring German
mouth snaffle

Eggbutt snaffle

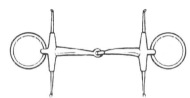

Fulmer cheek snaffle

Pelhams

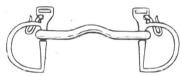

Kimblewick

Mullen mouth pelham

Put on the bridle by easing the bit
gently into the mouth with your
fingers.

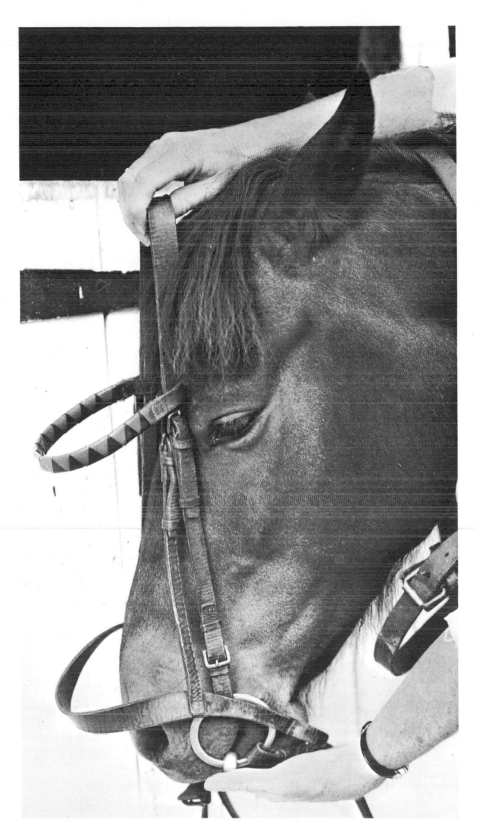

Saddles

A saddle that fits properly is vitally important and the reason for this is due to the construction of a pony's spine. The vertebrae, like our own, are a row of bones running from the skull to the tail but, unlike ours, each bone has what may be described as a vertical 'wing' resulting in a series of upright bones giving the effect of a fin on the back of a fish. This structure is embedded in muscle except along the central line of the back where it is just under the surface, and that is why weight must be kept off this part to avoid bruising.

Saddles are made on a beechwood frame called a 'tree', which is covered in stretched webbing and then padded so that it rests on either side of the pony's spine in a comfortable position just behind its shoulder-blades. It is shaped for two purposes: to fit the pony without putting incorrect pressure on its back or pinching the withers; and to fit the rider so that he sits well down in the saddle and is not pushed back when the lengths of the stirrup leathers are varied.

The Pony Club has designed a standard saddle pattern and makers using this pattern are allowed to mark them 'Pony Club Approved'. This type is ideal for general use and is helpful in establishing a correct seat for a young rider.

There are several special kinds of saddle, such as those used for show jumping, polo, dressage, showing, racing, and the side-saddle, the Western stock saddle and the Australian saddle. For all of them the same fundamental rule applies: the saddle must be securely and evenly placed on the animal's back and the rider must feel comfortable and secure, too.

To saddle a pony, put the saddle slightly forward on the withers and then slide it back to the correct position so that the hair is smoothed in the right direction under it. The front arch should be 2in (5cm) clear of the withers when the rider is mounted and the girths should come about 4in (10cm) behind the point of the pony's elbow. Buckle the girth so that it is not too tight but holds the saddle firmly, allowing enough room for your hand to be inserted flat under the girth. Check that the girth buckles are level, leaving three or more spare holes on each side to be taken up as necessary.

Girths are made from webbing, leather, nylon or string. Webbing is not a safe material as it deteriorates and may break without warning; leather is good provided that it is given constant care to keep it supple; nylon wears and washes easily but is inclined to slip; which leaves string as the best choice.

Stirrup irons vary in minor points but remain basically a tread with an arch above, through which the stirrup leather is looped. An iron must fit the rider's boot correctly or it becomes dangerous. This means that it should be large enough to leave a ½in (12mm) space on either side of the widest part of the boot to avoid the chance of it becoming jammed. Equally, an iron that is too large may allow a boot to slip right through, which can lead to a rider being dragged after a fall.

There are two types of safety stirrups. The Peacock pattern in which the outer

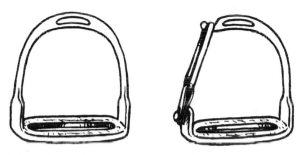

Stirrup irons: the standard type (*left*) and the safety iron.

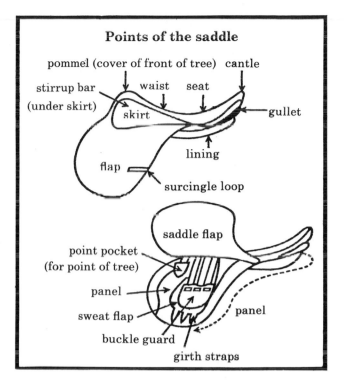

Points of the saddle

pommel (cover of front of tree)   cantle

stirrup bar
(under skirt)   waist   seat

skirt   gullet

flap   lining

surcingle loop

saddle flap

point pocket
(for point of tree)

panel

sweat flap   panel

buckle guard

girth straps

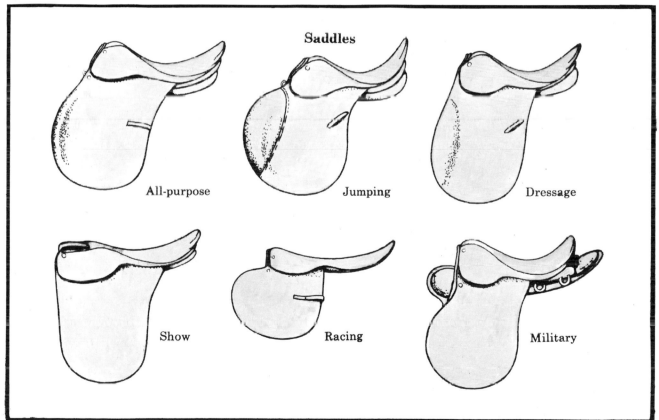

Saddles

All-purpose   Jumping   Dressage

Show   Racing   Military

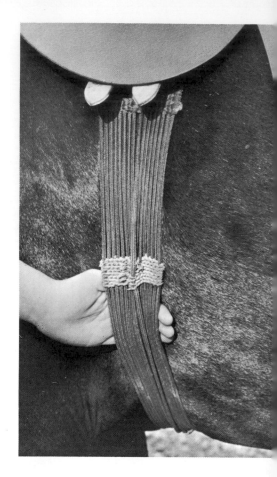

Saddling a pony the correct way. Put the saddle well forward on the withers and slide it back into position. *Right:* Check that the girth does not pinch the skin. *Below:* A leather-lined saddle, stirrup irons and leathers, a crupper and girths of string and of webbing.

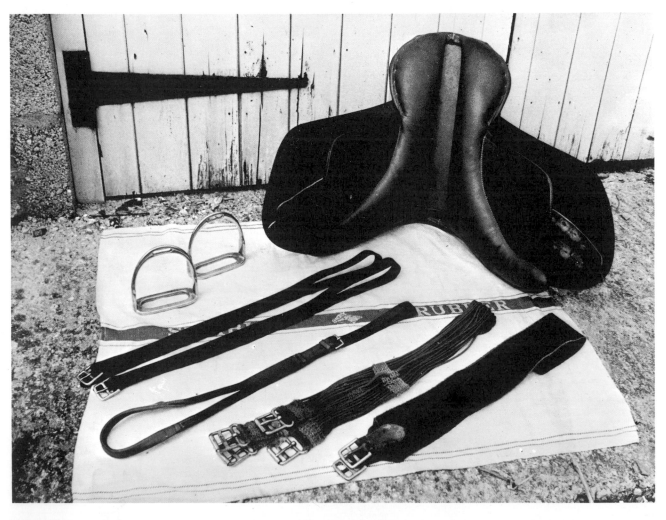

side of the metal arch is replaced by a rubber band is good, apart from the fact that the band may come undone at the wrong moment, and is inclined to perish and break after a time. The Australian Simplex iron is entirely metal and depends for its safety factor on a kink in the outer stem of the arch so that a boot comes out of the stirrup easily in an emergency.

Stirrups made of stainless steel are the best, as plated metal tends to chip and flake after a while and the softness of nickel means that it can bend.

Care of tack

The proper treatment of bridles and saddles means their preservation and this is most important from the point of view of safety, appearance and the expense involved in replacing neglected tack. Cleaning tack on the kitchen table and then hanging it up in the hall is not really satisfactory or likely to be popular with the rest of the household, and so if possible it is desirable to have a tack room adjoining the stable.

To furnish a tack room you need a shelf for cleaning materials and brackets and hooks for hanging up tack that is being cleaned and for 'putting up' (storing). It is possible to buy various specially made devices but these are expensive and a handy-man can make alternatives quite easily.

The largest item is a 'saddle-horse', which is really a sort of table on firm sturdy legs with a top that is shaped like the roof of a house instead of being flat. The saddle can be cleaned on this and then put up on a wall bracket which can be a peg or, better, an inverted V made by nailing two narrow pieces of plank edge to edge and mounting this on a shelf-bracket. It should be fixed firmly and measure about 18in (46cm) in length.

Ordinary screw hooks can be used for hanging stirrup irons and leathers and the girth, hooked by the metal buckle; but it is bad for the leather of a bridle to be dangled from a hook when it is put up, and here a half-sized empty food can is useful and can look smart. Punch a hole through the unopened end of the can, push a nail through this and then drive it home in a chosen place on the wall. The best sort of nail is of the type used for fixing corrugated roofing sheets which has a twisted shank and a mushroom-shaped head, as this holds well. Paint the tin black, while or any other colour with an enamel paint and the result is a tidy bridle bracket which few people will recognize as an old tin can.

If space permits, you should have a small table for cleaning parts of bridles and leather pieces other than saddles, but failing this a wide-hinged shelf will do. The maxim 'a place for everything and everything in its place' applies particularly in a tack room.

As to cleaning materials, these consist of saddle-soap, neatsfoot oil and metal polish, plus a couple of sponges, a chamois leather and various rags for use in cleaning and polishing. Many people also clean their boots in the tack room and, in that case, dubbin and boot-polish can be added to the list.

Above: A well-equipped
tack room.

Right: A kit for grooming
and for cleaning tack.

From top left, back row:
Horse shampoo, hoof oil,
kit box, two sponges.

Centre row: Sponge and
saddle soap, mane comb,
scissors, cactus cloth,
hoof pick, tail bandage
and metal polish.

Front row: Wisp on stable
rubber, body brush,
metal curry comb, plastic
curry comb, rubber curry
comb, water brush and
dandy brush.

70

Cleaning tack is a tedious chore, but can be made less so if you establish a routine. First place the saddle on the saddle-horse and remove the stirrup leathers and irons, sponge them clean with cold water and hang them up to dry. Lukewarm water can be used to clean sweat-stained stirrup leathers, but it is important to remember not to soak them and to wipe them dry before hanging up. Do the same with a leather girth, but a non-leather one should be hung up to dry and then brushed clean, apart from giving it a thorough wash once a week or so. Now turn to the saddle itself, again sponging with cold water under the flaps and also the lining if it is made of linen or leather. Those lined with serge should be brushed with a dandy brush.

While these items are drying the bridle can be dealt with. Take it to pieces and sponge each separate part with cold water. Wash the bit (and the curb chain if there is one) and dry all these parts of the bridle with a chamois leather.

Now return to the saddle, covering the whole surface of every leather part with saddle-soap, using less on the seat and flaps than elsewhere, as otherwise an excess may stain your clothes next time it is used. Wipe it over lightly with a dry rag and then put it up. Soap the stirrup leathers and leather girth, wipe them and put up, and, at the same time, wipe over the dry stirrup irons and then hook one by its top slit and place the other upside-down through it so that they hang together neatly.

Take each part of the bridle and rub lightly with saddle-soap, and polish the metal parts with a little metal polish on a dry cloth. Take care not to leave polish on the bit mouthpiece because your pony will not appreciate the taste. The leather pieces should be polished with a cloth but not to a high gloss as the important thing is to let the soap have its suppling and preservative effect. Now the bridle can be re-assembled and put up.

5 Learning to ride

Many people begin riding with the help of a quiet pony belonging to a friend, perhaps walking round a paddock, and this is not a bad way to start: it will give you the *feel* of riding. However, while it is possible for a self-taught rider to learn how to stay in the saddle, riding properly and with style so that you are good enough to enter show classes or a one-day event involves concentrated effort.

The first thing a novice has to remember is that a pony is a live animal and not a bicycle. It is very easy to be so concerned about yourself and what you ought to be doing that you forget that horsemanship means a close contact between pony and rider, so that the animal is happy and content to do what is asked of it. Apart from balance and grip, an understanding of the aids is vital. You ask a pony to go forward or stop by applying the appropriate aid or signal, and not by giving it a thump in the ribs with your heels or by leaning back on the reins. When you have learned to ride well in partnership with a pony, then you will really enjoy riding.

Mounting and dismounting

It is a wise precaution to ask someone to hold the pony while you learn how to get up into the saddle and down again, but, in any case, follow the correct routine by checking the girths and seeing that the stirrup irons are down. You are going to mount on the nearside – the left side of the pony – so you stand with your left shoulder to the pony's shoulder and with the reins in your left hand, which is placed on the withers in front of the saddle. Then, with the help of your right hand, put your left foot into the stirrup and press your toe down so that it comes under the girth; take hold of the front arch of the saddle with your right hand as you turn your body to face the pony, and then spring up, swinging your right leg over while taking care not to touch the pony's quarters. Come down into the saddle gently so that you do not thump on the pony's back, gather up the reins and place your right foot in the off-side stirrup.

You are now mounted. It seems a complicated performance but soon becomes easy with a little practice and a patient pony. When you mount without an assistant to steady the animal, you must be sure that you have the reins in contact with the pony's mouth, not tightly held but under your control, so that if it moves

72

Debbie Johnsey showing her young sister how to hold the reins.

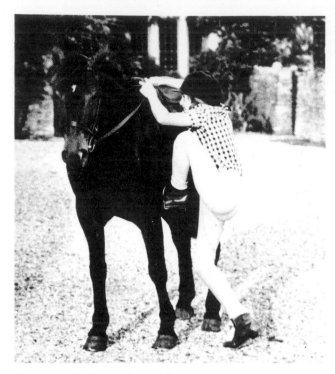

To mount: Hold on to the saddle, mane or neck strap. Place your left foot in the stirrup.

Spring up with the weight on your left leg.

Swing up and over with the right leg.

Lower your weight into the saddle gently.

Adjusting the stirrup
leather: the stirrups should
be as long as your arm from
armpit to fingertip.

for any reason you are able to halt it without hopping about on one leg—which can lead to an accident, besides looking silly.

To dismount, take both feet out of the stirrups, place your left hand on the pony's neck and the right on the pommel of the saddle, swing your right leg over its back and drop to the ground with both feet together. Land lightly on your toes, to avoid jarring, and away from the pony's front leg as an accidental kick will startle it.

Casual dismounting can be dangerous, so be sure that both feet are out of the stirrups. *Never* throw your right leg over the withers and drop down, because, in this position, you have lost the reins and so any control of the pony. A fall at this point could result in a nasty bang on the head, even though you have some protection in the form of a hard hat.

75

Stirrups

Learning to judge the correct length of stirrup is important. As a rule, this is done by measuring it against the length of your arm. Place your knuckles on the stirrup bar of the saddle and the stirrup iron in your armpit, which will arrive at a practical length to give the strongest seat without interfering with the use of the legs. A long stirrup has the advantage of allowing full use of your legs as aids, but also has the effect of weakening your seat and allowing you to fall forward, while short stirrups push the rider back in the saddle, again hindering the aids and, worse, putting weight on the pony's loins. The only advantage in this case is that you are not likely to fall forward with your thigh almost level.

Sitting down in the saddle has to be learned in order to gain a good seat, and this is often done by riding for short periods without stirrups. In this way you stretch the legs and feet down, which can be an uncomfortable exercise and a good way to get a stitch in your inside, but does result in a better, deeper seat and so the need to let down the stirrups a notch or two.

Jockeys ride with very short stirrups in flat races and even in steeplechases, relying almost entirely on balance, so that they can use their weight forward to help the horse as it stretches out at speed, but this style is not used outside racing.

The seat

Just as suppleness and balance are important in a well-schooled pony, a good seat is dependent on the rider's ability to balance and grip without being stiff. A supple rider will be in rhythm with the pony's action, keeping the correct position in the saddle by balance, but always alert to grip with the knees and thighs when necessary. Only practice can achieve this, and, meanwhile, a neck-strap should be fitted on the pony to give a novice assurance, because the reins must not be used to maintain balance.

A rider with a good seat sits down in the central part of the saddle, with a straight but supple body. The shoulders should be back and the head up, but, at the same time, wholly relaxed, because stiffness makes balance almost impossible.

The knee and thigh must lie against the saddle with a natural grip achieved by a downward and inward pressure just sufficient to assist balance, and to keep it in the event of an emergency, such as a sudden shy.

The lower part of the leg should hang lightly by the pony's side with the stirrup leather straight, and the ball of the foot should rest in the stirrup iron so that the ankle is free to flex with the movement of the pony. In this position, the heel will be at a slightly lower level than the toe, which should point to the front; riders who point their toes out lose proper contact between the knee and the saddle, while the opposite has the effect of stiffening the ankle and bringing the calf of the leg away from the pony's side. The attitude of a rider from head to toe must be comfortable, because any discomfort will result in stiffness.

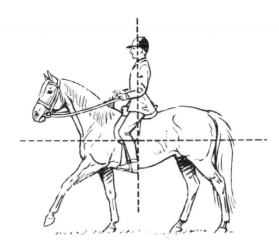

A good seat will maintain the rider's centre of gravity in line with that of the pony.

The upper arms should hang straight at the sides, not elbows out, the forearms bent to form a direct line through the reins to the pony's mouth, with the hands ready to respond gently to every movement of the animal's head and neck. Novice riders have a bad habit of jiggling the reins so that the pony gets a jab in its mouth with every step, whereas a rider with good hands will keep them still, just maintaining a soft contact with a pony which is comfortably on the bit.

Reins and hands

Nowadays the reins are usually held in both hands. Snaffle reins can pass either between the third and little fingers or under the little finger, to go through the lightly clenched hands and to be held between forefinger and thumb. In the case of a double rein bridle, the little finger of each hand should divide the reins.

Holding the reins correctly: in a straight line from the elbow, with thumbs uppermost and wrists relaxed.

Be sure that the snaffle (or bridoon) rein is on the outside, because a muddle with the reins can lead you to apply the curb when this is not needed. The use of double reins should really be left until the rider is reasonably experienced, because they require subtlety on the rider's part to be effective; two reins are a lot to cope with if you are a novice.

Hands holding the reins should be held about 4in (10cm) apart, thumbs uppermost, and just above and in front of the saddle pommel. This position allows gentle give-and-take with the natural movements of the pony, until a light touch is needed to convey an instruction. If too much or too little rein is held, then the rider will not be sitting correctly in the saddle.

In the early stages of learning to ride it is tempting to look on the reins alone as a means of turning and stopping your mount, but you have to realize that the hands are never used without the other signals from your back and legs: in fact, a proper use of the aids.

The aids

Anyone who is not well versed in the intricacies of advanced dressage may find that watching this kind of competition is rather boring (which is why it is seldom shown on television), but it can tell a young rider a lot about the subtle application of the aids as a well-schooled horse responds to almost unnoticeable signals. At the opposite extreme, a common sight at gymkhanas is a child mounted on a sullen pony, trying to propel it along by means of a rhythmic tattoo with the heels on its ribs. This looks ugly and achieves nothing beyond spoiling the temperament of a pony that may have been kind and willing at one time.

The aids are divided into two sections: natural aids and artificial aids. The natural aids are signals given by the rider's body with degrees of pressure from the legs and hands, occasionally reinforced by the voice. A straight but relaxed back leads to a correct seat, which in turn allows the legs to maintain control in conjunction with the reins. So, the whole body is involved in the proper use of natural aids.

A young rider schooling her mount, teaching obedience to the aids.

A pony being schooled under saddle.

Above: Half-circle to the right at walk.

Top, right: Circle right at sitting trot.

Right: Transition from trot to canter.
Practising these movements will improve the pony's impulsion and balance.

To respond properly the pony must be on the bit, so that there is continuous gentle contact between its mouth and your hands. It obeys a message from the reins by relaxing its jaw and must receive a corresponding relaxation of your hands as a reward, while your legs continue to signal for as long as necessary.

Beginning with the walk, the pony must be standing four square, on the bit and alert. You straighten in the saddle, ease the reins, still keeping light contact, and close your legs. To bring it back to the halt, increase the pressure of the legs slightly, and tighten the rein smoothly, releasing both pressures as the pony obeys by coming to a steady standstill. These simple aids will take you on into a canter or reduce the pace when they are used sympathetically to give commands that a pony understands.

A new pony may not respond to natural aids if it has been spoilt by a previous owner. In this case the aids can be reinforced by a *gentle* reminder with the whip to make it go forward until it learns to connect leg pressure with a light tap from the whip, and so begins to answer the correct aid.

In order to turn left or right, or circle in either direction, guide the pony with the appropriate rein while giving a little with the other rein to allow its head to move as the body turns. At the same time, apply the leg on the inner side of the turn or circle at the girth and your outer leg behind the girth to bring the pony's

79

Below: Stages of the walk.

Below, right: Stages of the trot. A pony walks in four-time and trots in two-time. It is important for the rider to be aware of the pony's natural movement, in order to adapt himself to it and improve it where necessary.

quarters round. Many ponies are stiffer on one side or the other, often because they have been lunged in only one direction, and can suffer muscular pain if forced into too small a circle; so take large circles until you know that the pony you are riding is supple, with well-muscled quarters. You will find more detailed advice on lungeing and the general schooling of both pony and rider in Chapter Seven (see pages 100–07).

These elementary natural aids are enough for the novice to master. Later, as your riding technique improves, it will be time to learn more advanced movements and the correct use of artificial aids.

Stages of the canter. This is a three-time gait with a moment of complete suspension (see last diagram in the sequence). The rider needs to learn how to feel which foreleg is leading.

Riding

Riding involves the rider in a rhythmic association with the action of the pony. At the walk this is nothing more than a slight sway as you sit erect in the saddle, but at the trot you should incline forward a little. Learning to rise in the saddle while trotting is a basic lesson which seems difficult at first, because the rider tries to push up and down independently instead of allowing the pony's rhythm to do it, assisted by the flexion of the knee and ankle joints. The complete novice tends to lean forward too far, with a stiff back, and so loses a proper seat and thus a sense of balance. This results in the reins being used as an anchor to the great discomfort of the pony, and the saddle pommel will provide another hand-hold for emergencies, but it is better to avoid becoming tense, because of nerves: if you relax and let the rhythm take you along, you will soon learn the rising trot so that it becomes automatic.

Cantering correctly is a most comfortable pace, when the rider is moving with the pony and sitting well down in the saddle so that there is no daylight between

81

A good collected canter with the rider sitting deep in the saddle.

it and the seat. Bumping is caused by a rigid back. To gallop, sit down in the saddle and push the pony on with your seat and legs until it is going freely; then transfer your weight to the knees and stirrups, so that it is off the saddle and your body leans forward over the hands. This change in the centre of your weight helps the pony at speed.

An important point to remember is that a pony must be able to stretch its neck so that its nose remains in front of its forefeet as speed increases. In order to do this it will need more rein while still maintaining contact with the rider's hands.

It is quite possible to teach yourself to ride to this extent with the kind co-operation of a quiet pony, but it is sensible to perfect your style and learn about your faults from a qualified teacher. A cine film taken by a relative or friend can be a great help, too, if it shows you riding at the walk, trot and canter in a paddock, since it is often a shock to find that you are habitually doing things the wrong way without realizing it. Work on the lunge rein is excellent training for both pony and rider, and this basic form of exercise is discussed in detail under 'Schooling' in Chapter Seven (see pages 100–04).

Applying further aids

At each stage when you are asking more from a pony you must first make sure that the animal is physically fit enough to perform the exercise, and that you are able to convey the necessary instructions so that the pony understands and is able to obey. Resistance and evasion by the pony will be your fault.

To rein back correctly the pony must be standing steady and relaxed on the bit; then apply both legs to send it up into the bit while retaining pressure with the reins, so that it moves back straight for the required number of steps in the reverse of the walk. To begin with, ask for only a few steps back before easing the reins to bring the animal to a smooth halt, and send it forward two strides or so, otherwise your pony might learn to go backwards as an evasion. Practise this movement only once or twice in any riding session.

To teach your pony the simple change of leg, that is, leading with the outside leg, which is vital if you intend to enter show classes for ridden ponies, you must be absolutely sure that it understands and is obedient to the aids you apply,

The exaggerated forward seat used in racing. All riders lean forward with their weight off the saddle when asking a pony to gallop. The rider should not, of course, be hatless!

83

because otherwise you are going to get into a muddle. The first essential is to teach canter-to-walk without any resistance. To achieve this, canter in a large circle making sure the pony is leading on the correct leg, the inside leg. Use your back and seat aids in addition to closed legs and pressure on the reins, which will bring the pony's hind legs under it until it can pass straight into a walk. This will take several lessons to accomplish without an intermediate trotting stage.

When this has been learned, and accepted obediently by the pony, you can try the change of leg in the centre of a figure of eight, which involves canter-to-walk and then striking off into a canter again on the opposite leg. To achieve this, and assuming a change to the right fore-leg leading, use the right rein to bend the pony slightly to the right. Then, applying pressure with both your legs, the left to the rear of the right on the girth impel the animal into a canter again. At first the intervening walk should be over some distance, which is gradually reduced as the pony understands what is required. You should learn to feel which leg is leading by the action of the pony's shoulder, because glancing down to check looks amateurish in the show-ring and will be noted by the judge.

Artificial aids

Whips, spurs and martingales are classed as artificial aids but are seldom applied to a well-schooled pony. The whip is carried as part of the equipment of a rider, to be used on rare occasions and then with varying degrees of smartness behind the girth, as a reminder to the pony that it must concentrate and not 'play up'; but, first of all, be sure that the animal is not frightened or bewildered or just feeling jolly, and that you are not in a bad temper.

Anyone who has taught a foal to lead on a halter will know that the lightest of touches behind the saddle area will send it forward, because the hide of a pony is extremely sensitive, and so there is never any excuse for hitting one hard. At the same time, most intelligent animals will see how far they can go without a reprimand, and you must remain in control to get anywhere with training a pony.

Spurs are also more for adornment than use, and should be of the plain, curved-neck type, always worn pointed downwards. Spurs with rowels are not used these days, when ponies are trained and not 'broken' as they were in years gone by. If spurs are used as an aid to reinforce leg pressure, they are applied gently against the pony's side and *never* with the toe outwards so that the point of the spur is used. Spurs should not in any case be worn by novice riders.

Martingales are of three main types: the *standing*, *running* and *Irish martingale*. The object of all three is to control a pony that tends to carry its head high and so above the angle of the rider's control. Choosing the type of martingale, and fitting it properly, to correct a certain fault is a job for an expert, because otherwise more harm than good will result.

84

The elements of dressage

There is no doubt that all riding ponies can benefit from some dressage training. The object, quite simply, is to make a pony, or horse, more efficient as a working partner, whether in the hunting field or show-jumping, because it will become obedient, supple and balanced.

If it is trained sympathetically, an intelligent pony will learn to enjoy

Simple schooling movements for work on the flat in an enclosed area.

1 Turn down the centre line to change the rein.

2 Turn across the school to change the rein.

3 Single shallow loop.

4 Inverted loop followed by changing the rein into the corner.

5 Three loops of the serpentine.

6 Incline across the school.

7 Large circle.

8 Changing the rein out of the circle (figure of eight).

9 Changing the rein within the circle.

10 Half circle and incline back to the track.

11 Turn down centre line and incline back to the track.

12 Half circle across the school.

Shoulder-in to the right and the left helps to achieve better impulsion and makes the pony's spine supple.

performing dressage movements, but it must be brought to each stage by degrees, understanding and responding obediently to the aids, while it improves in physical condition with exercise, daily lessons and correct feeding. The end product is then a pony that is 'collected', which means that its body is flexible from head to tail, with the hindquarters impelling the animal forward with good action from the hocks.

However, dressage training is not something that a novice should attempt alone, because an inexperienced rider can soon ruin a promising pony, which, confused by vague or muddled instructions, will resort to evasion–becoming stubborn or even rearing. The best place for a rider and a pony to learn simple dressage movements is in a covered school under the guidance of a qualified instructor, who will insure that the correct aids are given and that the pony is not forced beyond its capacity.

Great importance is attached to lateral movements as a suppling exercise, which involve training your pony to walk in two tracks; the front legs tread one step to the side of the line taken by the hind legs. Once this has been accepted, it then continues as an exercise at the trot. This is known as the 'shoulder-in' and is performed to the right and left. The aim is to bend the spine which, in turn, makes the hocks flex and brings them under the pony to obtain better impulsion, and, when the spine has become supple on both sides, encourages straight action.

Impulsion is vital in show-jumping and this means that the hocks must be well under to achieve the necessary 'spring' effect. Apart from the shoulder-in, a 'half-halt' exercise is used for this purpose. This uses the aids to indicate that the

86

The classic jumping position. The rider's forward seat, together with the slightly shortened stirrup irons, enable the weight of the rider to be taken off the pony's back and absorbed at the knee and into the stirrup irons.

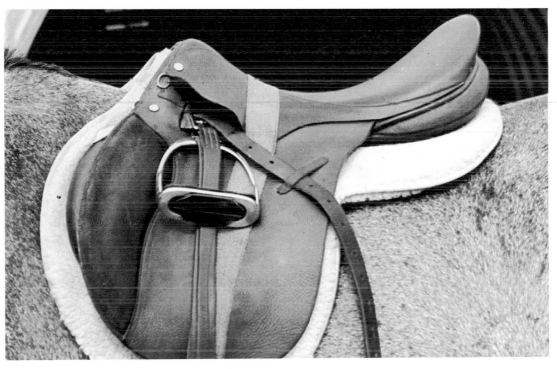

A good jumping saddle, firmly secured by a surcingle that will prevent the saddle from slipping while jumping.

87

pony is going to be asked to reduce speed or halt, when it will answer by starting to brake, but is then taken on again. Obviously, this lesson must be given clearly to avoid confusing the pony.

Once a pony is reasonably supple it can progress to the counter-canter with the help of a qualified instructor. Only do this gradually because it involves a good deal of strain at first, since it is contrary to normal action, but is valuable to gain suppleness and balance. This is achieved by taking a serpentine course at the canter with the pony bent slightly to the right and leading with that leg, so that when the course curves to the left the right leg is still leading with the body bent in the same direction. This exercise is performed to both right and left, but must not be overdone until the pony is thoroughly trained to it.

When you and your pony have learned the halt, walk, trot, canter and rein-back, and progressed to shoulder-in, half-halt and counter-canter, you are well on the way to becoming a good rider; while the pony has acquired the habit of obedience, and a muscular, supple frame, which will make jumping easier.

Learning to jump

Confidence is the foundation of good jumping in both rider and pony. It is just as important not to over-face yourself, that is, not to jump beyond your capacity, because then you will transmit nervousness to the pony, which may suspect that the jump is worse than it looks and so refuse or run out.

In order to jump fluently a pony must balance itself at the approach to the obstacle, lowering its head and stretching its neck, and judging the distance and take-off point by looking at the ground-line at the base of the fence. The normal and easiest take-off point will be the same distance from the fence as its height—for example, a pony jumping a 2ft (61cm) practice fence will commence the jump 2ft (61cm) before it. As the animal gathers itself and leaves the ground, the neck shortens as the forehand lifts, and then stretches again as the body springs upwards and forwards with hocks tucked up. There is then a moment when the pony is in mid-air, its neck fully extended, until it lands with head up and neck shortened again.

These changing attitudes in the course of a jump taking a matter of seconds demand careful handling of the reins so that, while contact is maintained, there is no risk of jabbing the pony's mouth. For this reason a neck-strap offering a handhold will be helpful.

The jumping position of the rider is very similar to that adopted at the gallop, except for the seat which should be close to but not on the saddle. Your weight is on the thigh and knee down to the heel, so you must have a good saddle that really fits the pony comfortably, and allows you to sit securely with enough leather on the forward part for your knees. The stirrups may be shortened slightly for jumping, provided that this does not result in a tendency to stand up, when your balance will be lost.

88

An energetic take-off:
Debbie Johnsey jumps on
her pony, Mystery, at
Hickstead.

A snaffle bit should be used for practice jumping. Your shoulders, arms and hands must be ready to give and take as the pony moves its head in the course of a jump; and you must let the reins slip through your fingers if you feel that you are being left behind, using the neck-strap to regain your balance, and so avoid a jab in the pony's mouth while you slide back towards its loins.

Top show-jumping riders often 'fly up' as the horse jumps but this is an expert performance, combining timing and balance, and a novice who attempts such a style is likely to fly further and part company with their pony on the way!

First attempts at training for jumping are best made over poles on the ground. The pony can trot over these without interrupting its stride. A single cavalletto makes a good first jump (see Chapter Seven, page 104), approached at a steady canter, as this is the easiest pace for the rider who has taken up the jumping position, leaning forward slightly, in anticipation of the jump. Later on you will be able to sit down in the saddle to place the pony and maintain its impulsion up to the fence and then automatically gain the correct position on take-off. A pony easily becomes tired of jumping if it is asked to go over the same fence time and again, but is more likely to 'hot up' if it has a line to jump, so it is better to arrange several cavalletti in various parts of the paddock and approach them from different directions.

All paces should be practised over cavalletti, logs and small ditches, before progressing to larger fences. At this stage it is worth considering the layout of a jumping area in the paddock, as the ground is important and, at one extreme, the chosen place may make perfect going in the winter but become rock hard in summer, or, in the opposite case, can be a marsh in winter.

A variety of fences are needed to give you and the pony all-round experience, and should include poles, single and parallel; brush fences; a bank; a small simulated gate; one or two solid fences of rough poles; and, ideally, a water ditch. Practice over these will prepare both of you for hunting and show-jumping alike. Further practice in a covered school over conventional fences, with the advice of

89

Work over ground rails at all paces helps to develop calmness and rhythm as well as strengthening the pony's back muscles. Here we see the walk on a loose rein, which encourages the rounding and lowering of the head and neck.

Trotting over ground rails is the next stage, once a regularly paced walk has been achieved.

This shows the non-jumping stride before a spread fence. The pony must lower its head and stretch its neck to judge the distance correctly.

A parallel fence. This can be jumped from both sides. With a ground-line at the base of the fence, the novice pony will find it easier to calculate the right take-off point.

The take-off over a parallel fence. Here the ground-line has been removed since the pony and rider have learnt to gauge the distance.

The same jump, but this time the picture shows the period of suspension. Notice the way in which the pony tucks under its fore feet to avoid hitting the second bar.

A jump over telegraph poles. It is important to get your pony used to different jumps in preparation for hunting or the cross-country phase of eventing.

an instructor, will advance your training if you hope to take up show-jumping seriously.

In the early stages it is a good idea to give the pony a definite ground-line at the base of a jump, and this can be a low-set cavalletto or a row of hedge trimmings, but it is a mistake to get to the point of relying on a ground-line to judge the take-off since they will not be available out hunting or at all competition fences.

Many people build practice fences too high. The height for an average pony should be about 2ft (61cm), asking for more effort by increasing the spread with parallel poles rather than by making the fence higher. It is much better to provide a home course that a pony will jump unerringly, because in the excitement of the hunting field or a competition it will jump bigger fences with confidence acquired from careful schooling and its sense of trust and obedience.

Refusals and running out may be due to several causes, but the main ones are over-facing and a rider who shortens the stride too much on the approach and presents the pony to a fence badly so that it loses confidence in its ability to jump. A pony with a sore mouth or legs will also refuse, and so will one that is unfit. If none of these reasons apply, then you must show determination and resort to

92

A fine jump over the water. This is Debbie Johnsey in one of her first shows. Notice the forward position of the rider and her light but controlled hold on the reins.

smaller fences until the pony will jump willingly. As always, a qualified instructor, who can watch what you and the pony are doing, will help to cure faults at their outset.

Since it would be very unwise for a novice to learn how to ride with a 'green' pony, it may seem odd to lay so much emphasis on schooling the pony through your stages of learning, but you have to get to know one another by degrees to make a working partnership, and this is the best way. Even when you have become an expert rider, any new mount ought to be schooled from the beginning so that you gain mutual understanding.

6 Riding with friends

Hacking in the country or even in city parks is a pleasant occupation and gives the pony and rider exercise which they both need if they are to work well together. However, riding out inevitably involves travelling on public roads for some part of the time and so it is important to understand the Road Traffic Act where it applies to animals, and also to know the unwritten country code of behaviour which is expected of people on horseback.

Riders must keep to the left with the traffic in urban areas, keeping well in to the side of the road but not straying on to a footpath except in an emergency. Animals are not allowed on motorways. In the country, 'Keep Left' still applies on most roads, but in lanes and byways it may be safer to travel on the right for some part of the way if, for instance, that side gives better visibility, as in the case of a series of left-hand bends. When a group of people are riding together they must travel in single file and not in twos and threes.

While riders have a duty not to obstruct traffic unnecessarily, motorists must abide by common-sense rules and they are not allowed to sound the car horn, rev the engine or cut in on ridden or led animals. In addition, they must slow down and, if requested to do so, stop in order to allow a nervous pony to be ridden past or taken in to a gateway. However, if you are riding a pony on the highway it is not safe to assume that every driver will follow the rules, but when they do, a smile and polite thanks are in order.

If you are riding one pony and leading another, again, keep to the left with the led pony on your left, but when leading a pony on foot walk on the right with the pony on your right. Incidentally, *never* ride a bicycle while leading a pony.

The unwritten rules of behaviour are questions of common sense and politeness. In places set aside for riding, such as bridle-paths, horsemen have the right of way, but even in these places you must be prepared to slow and avoid wandering children or short-sighted people. Equally, while it is possible to ride on some footpaths in the country these are set aside for walkers and so a rider must allow them right of way. Some country rides and bridle-paths are intersected by gates and these must be shut after you have gone through; and if part of the way skirts a cultivated field or a hay meadow then keep to the edge. Lastly, country people expect a word in passing and a cheerful 'Good morning'

When riding in the country, always remember the country code.

94

and a chat about the weather is not only a courtesy but may give you a bonus of information about other places where you will be allowed to ride.

Short rides

A short ride in this context would be, say, two hours of varied exercise with part of the time spent at walking pace. Trotting should not be faster than seven or eight miles (11–13km) an hour and you should bear in mind that travelling downhill at the trot puts a strain on the pony's forelegs. At intervals you should change diagonals by bumping once in the saddle and rising as the other foreleg touches the ground; this relieves any possible strain on the legs, particularly on hard ground.

After the first mile check the girth and tighten it if necessary. A pony will often expand its rib cage at saddling time but returns to normal size as it settles down to enjoy the outing.

Make use of grass verges and other soft ground for cantering and galloping (but take care the grass does not conceal a ditch), always remembering that a pony is as good as its legs and percussion on a hard road is likely to damage them. The last mile home should be covered at a walk, so that your pony is brought home from exercise in a cool and calm state.

All this is what might be described as the technical side of a short ride, which will mean that the pony gains the maximum benefit from the exercise, while you enjoy the ride for its own sake with the companionship of friends who go out with you. Ponies are sociable animals and like to go out with one or more of their kind for company, just as we do. In common with most domestic animals they also like to hear the human voice, as you will see by the movement of a pony's ears while you are in conversation.

Riding in the country with a group of friends is fun for both pony and rider.

A short ride is an end in itself, unless it can include a visit to a neighbouring farm to enquire about hay supplies or to the village stores to leave a shopping list, but a well-planned long ride can be greater fun.

Long rides

A long ride suggests a picnic at the end of a journey of about eight or ten miles (13–16km), making a round trip of twenty miles (32km) in the day. Both ponies and their riders need to have been conditioned beforehand if the road home is not to be a weary drag, and it is wise to plan the trip either with a map or by choosing a place and going there by known ways. Otherwise it may be difficult to find a suitable site for the picnic, and time and hunger will leave you no alternative but the roadside, chewing sandwiches and wondering where to find water for the ponies.

If, without trespassing, you can find a place with a stream, shade and fairly sparse grass this will be ideal. Then on arrival you can allow the pony a reasonable drink (not too much), and a small feed of cubes. Let it graze and rest quietly while you eat your meal. These surroundings can be found in the National Parks and some areas of common land, but elsewhere, where the countryside has been taken over by agricultural farmland, it is better to ask permission before settling down to a picnic on private land.

Apart from planning the journey, there are other preparations to make before starting out. First of all, the pony needs a drink and a small net of hay about an hour before you have your own breakfast, and then before saddling-up should be groomed and have its feet picked out. Put on a halter under the bridle so that you can unbridle your pony to let it graze. Measure out about 1lb (500g) of cubes and put in a plastic or cloth bag ready to take for the pony's midday feed.

Your own picnic is a matter of taste but keep it simple. Sandwiches can be wrapped in greaseproof paper or plastic film; chocolate is nice but unlikely to travel well on a warm day, so fruit (apples or bananas) is preferable. Thermos flasks of hot drinks are not practicable and a plastic, screw-topped bottle of lemonade or similar soft drink is the answer. But, whatever you take, do not carry it in metal, glass or hard plastic containers, because these can be dangerous if you have a fall. For the same reason, if you carry a knife it should be a clasp-knife. It is a good idea to take a hoof pick with you, and a bit of money for phone calls as well as ice creams.

Nowadays few people own saddle-bags. The alternative is to tie your own food in a neat parcel to the D ring at one side of the front of your saddle and the bag of pony cubes on the opposite side. Or you can wear some form of satchel and carry both parcels in that; but aim at simplicity and avoid setting forth looking like the White Knight in *Alice Through the Looking Glass*.

In the course of the ride your priority should be the welfare of your pony, saving effort whenever possible. This means dismounting when standing still for

97

It will help your pony to relax and put lessons into practice if you go for a quiet hack after a schooling session.

any time, and, every now and again, leading the pony with the girth slackened, particularly up hills. Assuming that your journey has been leisurely, you will arrive at the picnic site after about two hours, when the pony can be unsaddled and its back slapped and massaged to restore the circulation.

Riding in the country for no particular purpose is a very pleasant occupation, allowing time to look at scenery which would flash past a car window and enabling you to see more wild-life at close quarters than would be possible on foot, because normally shy creatures pay little attention to a pony walking by.

While riding out from home necessarily limits the area you can travel around,

this can be extended if you own, or can borrow, a trailer and so be transported with your pony to a National Park or forestry land where riding is permitted — arranging to be picked up at the point of departure at a suitable time.

Long rides of this kind are the best means of getting the pony and yourself in condition for hunting or other strenuous pursuits, including organized endurance riding.

The stables at a Pony Club camp. A holiday at one of these camps will teach you how to look after your pony better, as well as giving you plenty of opportunity for improving your riding and generally having fun.

Camping

In most places it is difficult for a small party to camp with ponies. The idea seems fun but in reality a great deal of organization is essential, and so the best way to camp is as a member of your local branch of the Pony Club.

These camps cater for you and your pony, provide instruction in horsemanship and amusements such as mounted games, and offer the companionship of people of your own age with the same interests. You can find out about the local Pony Club from the Secretary of the local pack of foxhounds or from the British Horse Society's headquarters at Stoneleigh. The American Pony Club is affiliated to the British one. In Australia the Pony Club Council (Sec: F. J. Kennedy, c/o Royal National Agricultural and Industrial Association of Queensland, Exhibition Ground, Gregory Terrace, 4006 Brisbane) or the Equestrian Federation (Royal Show Ground, Epsom Road, Ascot Vale, 3032) and, in New Zealand, the Pony Club Association (Sec: Mrs F. H. Bond, Lockwood Road, Palmerston North) will provide information and addresses.

7 Riding in competitions

In the course of the spring and summer there are about two thousand events in Britain which include classes for ponies, ranging from village gymkhanas and county agricultural shows to the Royal International Horse show in London, and, among these, there are chances for the all-round handy pony just as much as for the show pony. Success or failure in competitions of any kind is directly related to the amount of work done at home. If you are prepared to train your pony and yourself, there are rosettes waiting to be pinned on the tack-room wall.

Most people begin competition riding in local gymkhanas, and this is a very good training ground where the pony and rider learn to perform in public all that they have practised in a paddock at home or with the Pony Club.

Assuming that your pony is a moderate animal it will still be able to match one of better breeding in a show if it is eager but obedient, well turned out and expertly handled so that it catches the judge's eye as a pony with a suitable temperament for a child to ride. However, in this case, it must have a nice small head and good conformation and action (see Glossary) to reach the top, whereas in a gymkhana or jumping competition it is the combined ability of the pony and rider that gains points.

The whole secret of training ponies lies in persuading them to work willingly, and to achieve this they must feel both affectionate and respectful, trusting that your demands are not beyond their capabilities. If your pony does not respond as it should, the fault in all probability is yours—allowing for the fact that all ponies in the peak of condition have bouts of mischievousness. Resistance of any kind generally stems from bewilderment, because instructions have not been given clearly, and a refusal at a jump usually means lack of training, wrong presentation, or over-facing. So always check yourself before blaming the pony.

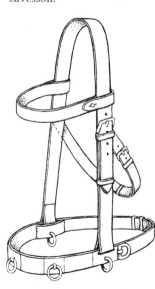

A lightweight lungeing cavesson.

Schooling

Lungeing is the foundation of good schooling. It consists of exercising a pony in a circle round the trainer on a lungeing rein attached to a cavesson, which is a headpiece fitted with a leather-lined metal noseband carrying three swivel rings. The rein, obtained from any saddler, should be about 25ft (8m) long and is best

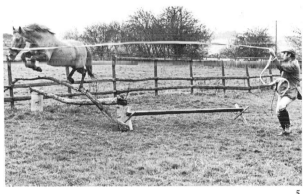

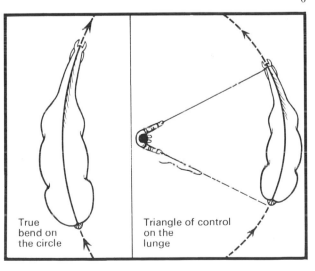

Above: Progressive stages in work on the lunge.

1 The pony or young horse is first led round the trainer by an assistant.

2 The assistant moves to a position inside and slightly behind the circling horse.

3 A good, free trot with the horse moving well forward.

4 Crossing a low grid of logs or cavalletti is a valuable balancing exercise: here the pony is led before being sent down the grid at the full length of the lunge rein.

5 A jump in excellent style over an improvized obstacle.

6 The pony stands square at halt on the circle. In all these movements the trainer must maintain sympathetic contact by the lunge rein.

True bend on the circle

Triangle of control on the lunge

101

A first lungeing lesson. The pony wears a cavesson and brushing boots.

Lungeing over poles is a useful introduction to jumping.

attached to the centre ring on the noseband, so that the pony can be circled in either direction without changing the rein from one side to the other. A long whip is necessary as an aid, applied very gently, to reinforce spoken commands.

The main objects of lungeing are to instil obedience and to muscle up the pony, which must be circled to both right and left to avoid developing muscles on one side only. At the same time, the trainer is able to see how the pony moves at the walk, trot and canter, and can, to some extent, remedy faults in action in the course of exercises.

If a pony is not accustomed to lungeing it will be necessary for a second person to lead it at first, walking on the outside so that it is the trainer who is in control, giving commands and making sure that the pony is never afraid of the whip but will respond to it. The long rein is essential since circling on a short one will not only defeat your purpose of improving the pony, but can cause it discomfort and alter its natural paces for the worse.

Working an animal successfully on a lunge rein is not easy and you will need advice and help from an experienced person to begin with, but it is surprising how quickly a pony will learn to work obediently on the lunge if it is given clear instruction from the first. As always, get one thing right before you progress to another; in this case, begin with the pony standing quietly, then give the command 'walk on' in a firm tone. Let it go round once or twice at this pace before telling it 'whoa', and keep at this, patiently but firmly, until the pony answers with obedience to these two commands. This is both concentrated work and rather boring for the animal, so five minutes should be the limit—ending the lesson at a moment when the pony has responded obediently. Then walk up to it, gathering in the rein as you go, and make much of it. Do not let the pony come in to you because that can teach it to break in from the circle while working. Titbit prizes are a mistake, too, as an intelligent pony will start to expect a prize at regular intervals and fail to think about its work.

The next stage is the trot, achieved by the command 'trot on' and encouraged, if necessary, by a slight flick of the whip in the air behind the hocks. Bring the pony back to a walk, trot again, then walk and stop for the day. Commands meant to slow the action should be spoken quietly with the word drawn out, while those for a quicker pace are said in a sharper voice, without either mumbling or shouting.

Once the pony is going forward at a free trot on the lunge it will begin to benefit from the exercise, learning to balance in the various paces, stretching its neck which will improve in muscle and so in shape, and suppling the body, especially along the back. The improvement to be seen after a week or two on the lunge is surprising, but lungeing must not be overdone—a gradual build-up to lessons lasting twenty minutes should be the maximum.

When you are certain of obedience, progress to a canter on the lunge, being careful not to allow the pony to hot up and spoil its previous good behaviour. Then revert to the walk, this time over a pole laid on the ground. Lay out further

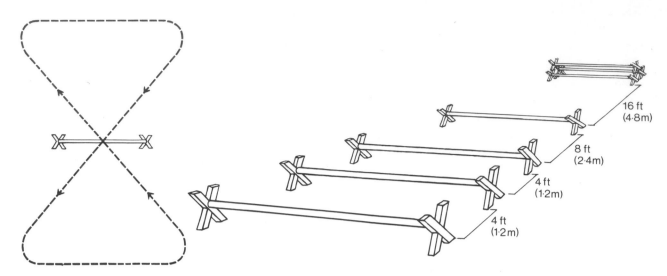

Above: A single cavalletto can be ridden on a figure of eight.

Above, right: Cavalletti set at the correct distances apart with a practice jump at one end. The intervals will vary according to the length of the pony's stride, but this rough guide shows the relative distances. This arrangement will encourage the pony to take off at the right distance from the fence itself, and will help to stop it rushing the fences.

poles as the pony learns to step over them calmly, matching their distance apart to the pony's stride so that there is no chance of it stumbling. As the next stage, trot over the poles, first one and then more, making sure that they are correctly placed.

Cavalletti are the most useful possession. Briefly, these consist of a 9ft (2.7m) pole with two pieces of 3in (7.62cm) square timber, 3ft (92cm) in length jointed together to form an X and attached at either end of the pole, which is fitted into one of the triangles of the X. By turning the crossed end-pieces, the pole can be at its lowest level of 10in (25cm) from the ground, raised halfway it will be 15in (38cm), and, lying across the top, be at a full height of 19in (48cm).

If you can have four, or better still, six cavalletti made up, they will be invaluable as you progress with lungeing exercises, as well as for jumping practice. The wooden poles can be painted in alternate stripes of red or blue and white, so that they are clearly visible to the pony, which must be introduced to them carefully so that it will step over without fuss—using the 10in (25cm) level at the walk.

After this course of training a pony will be much more supple and obedient under saddle, which is the next phase in getting it, and yourself, fit to enter competitions with confidence. To start with, repeat the series of lessons in the same order so that the pony understands that it must behave in the same manner while you are riding—always taking care to finish the lesson before it becomes bored and fidgety.

The next stage is trotting over cavalletti, set low, in a series laid out at about 4ft (1m) intervals, depending on the size of the pony and its stride. Then advance to jumping these, increasing the distance between the cavalletti, with variations such as putting two side by side to widen the jump or making four into a box formation with the square allowing room for one or two strides between hopping in and out. Variety will make the pony think better and prevent both of you from becoming bored.

104

Cavalletti are often made so that they can be stacked up to make higher jumps of various shapes and sizes, and this type is in common use; but stacking needs care because a pony trying to scramble its way out of a misjudged jump in the midst of a stack may injure itself or the rider. For this reason, cavalletti should be used singly and higher jumps made by balancing poles between two barrels, bearing in mind that, if you are to jump seriously, you will eventually need some practice jumps of the kind that you will meet in the show-ring.

While these exercises, including jumping, make a pony fit, supple and obedient, there is more work to be done under saddle. A pony must be taught to

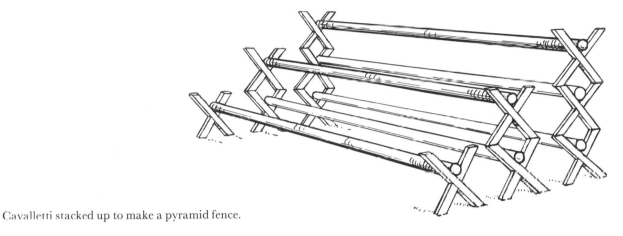

Cavalletti stacked up to make a pyramid fence.

The take-off of a good jump, well controlled, over two cavalletti. This is an advanced jump and care must be taken not to present an inexperienced pony with too difficult an obstacle; at best the pony might take fright and refuse and, at worst, it might injure itself in a fall.

105

Poles balanced between two barrels with a ground-line. Notice how hard both pony and rider are concentrating.

halt properly, standing four square and well balanced, ready to move off when the correct aid is applied—which is a slight pressure from your legs.

Walking comes next. The pony should walk out but not so quickly as to lose its natural pace. Then, when asked, it should go into a free, well-balanced trot; going on to a stronger trot by increasing its stride and not by going faster and higher like a hackney, when natural rhythm and balance will be lost. Rhythm and balance are just as important in the canter, which must be straight and effortless, and capable of a smooth increase in pace without hotting-up.

In each pace the rider must maintain a light contact with the pony's mouth, so that it is always on the bit, and apply the correct aids gently but firmly enough to make the signals clear to the animal.

Reining-back is often the most difficult lesson to teach so that a pony can do it correctly, and it is wise to leave this until last, when the pony will halt on the bit, balanced and ready to move. Then, by means of the reins and firm pressure of the legs, get it moving back three or four steps at first, relaxing your leg pressure but keeping the feel on the reins as the pony answers your instruction. It must learn to step back steadily and straight in the show-ring.

After completing this course of simple training a pony will be ready to enter in a gymkhana or a show-saddle class; but still has a good deal to learn before it is ready for show-jumping or cross-country events. Some of this basic work may

106

seem technical and complicated, but it is well worth the effort to achieve a well-mannered eager pony, rather than having one that slops around neither knowing or caring much about what it is supposed to be doing—and, of course, you will be a better rider and find more enjoyment in riding.

Gymkhanas

Entering a gymkhana can be great fun and many famous riders began their careers by taking part in them when they were children. Some of the best are organized by a local Pony Club branch with competitions for individuals and teams, either made up from among their own members or competing against teams from other branches. The top six teams in Britain end up in the final of the Prince Philip Cup at the Horse of the Year Show in London, to put on a display of riding in mounted games which is very popular with the audience.

However, it must be said that some people are not keen on gymkhanas because they believe that some of the competitions encourage both bad riding and the rough treatment of ponies, and this is sadly true on occasion, which is a point to remember.

There are dozens of different events for a gymkhana committee to choose from, but most of these involve three types of effort on the part of the pony and rider, which can be practised at home. Bending may be taken as the first example, since it is a straight-forward race in and out of a line of poles and back again to the finish, and this can be set up easily in your own paddock. Rather than driving poles into the ground, it is simpler to set the bases in concrete by standing, say, ten thick bamboo or similar poles in metal cans, filling the cans to the brim with concrete and arranging supports to hold the poles upright until the concrete is

A pony needs to be an all-round performer to do well in a gymkhana. Here we see a spirited pony moving quickly, obedient to the rider's commands.

107

hard. These will then stand on their own when required and can be stored away when not in use.

Bending means a fast getaway, a supple pony which can dart in and out of the poles, and make a quick turn to get back to the finish. Fit ponies enjoy this game and soon learn the rules, so that they need little guidance in the course of a bending race. There are several variants of the same kind of game; some involve the rider in dismounting to collect an item before racing back to the finish, and so it pays to teach your pony to stop and stand by a bucket while you dismount and mount again.

Unaccustomed sights and sounds, such as applause, can unnerve a novice pony, but, there again, home work will soon cure this if it is shown coloured flags (made from any remnants of red or white cloth), and hears pebbles dropped into a bucket. Introduce everything to it slowly and sympathetically, so that is realizes that there is nothing to fear and comes to accept all sorts of noises and strange objects as part of the day's work.

108

A bending race at a gymkhana near Canberra in Australia. The rider has to gallop down the line of bending posts, passing them on alternate sides, turn round the last post and retrace the course back to the finish.

Australian Pony Club competitors carry their buckets of water with care as they race over cavalletti.

Learning that it must trot calmly at your side, without shying away or pulling back, while you try to scamper along in a sack, is the third important lesson, and then you will have a very promising gymkhana pony.

In order to learn more about gymkhanas yourself it is well worth obtaining a booklet, *Mounted Games and Gymkhanas*, published by the British Horse Society, which describes numerous games and will enable you to find details of a particular game listed in a schedule, so that you can practise beforehand if it is new to you and your pony. Also go to several gymkhanas and watch others, so that you can learn from their victories and mistakes before competing yourself.

The show pony

Classes for ridden ponies in all but very minor shows are held under the rules of the British Show Pony Society, which imposes various regulations, and usually offers rosettes to the winners. The rider has to be a member of the Society in order

to compete and the pony must be registered with them. At some larger shows the first and second prizewinners may qualify for the Horse of the Year Show, which must be the goal of anyone with ambition, but the fact remains that there are very few top-class show ponies and those that exist are worth a mint of money. The average owner of a well-made pony, which has been fed, groomed and schooled to bring it into the ring at its best, should take pride in winning prizes at less grand events in the knowledge that this success is the fruit of their own hard work and 'know-how'.

To be worth showing, a pony must have good conformation and this begins with a quality head, because a large plain one will overrule any other good points about the rest of its body. An attractive pony has a small head, large kind eyes and a nice expression of friendly interest (perhaps it will seem odd to include facial expression as an asset in an animal, but neither a person nor a pony appears at their best if they are looking bored and sullen). The ears should be small; lop-ears are often a sign of a genuine horse or pony for no reason that anyone has explained, but they have no place in the show-ring.

The neck is important. It should be reasonably long and slightly arched, since a so-called 'ewe neck' is both ugly and a sign of weakness, as it results from a lack of muscle. Sometimes it can be improved by schooling in a pony which habitually carries its head too high with its nose stuck out. A good front is essential, with a long sloping shoulder and plenty of chest room, because front legs 'out of one hole' indicate a narrow chest that restricts the lungs and heart.

Opposite: A popular gymkhana event – the bending race. The better schooled your pony, the more nippily will you be able to weave past the poles.

Right: Pollyanna, a famous show pony and perhaps one of the most beautiful ponies ever bred.

111

Above: An exquisite pony yearling with a great future, and *(above right)* a Thoroughbred pony stallion: two examples of near-perfect conformation.

The body must be compact and deep, with a short back and well-developed quarters; the tail should be set fairly high, as a low-set tail is often combined with weak sloping quarters and 'cow-hocks' (the points of the hocks turning inwards), which are all signs of weakness. The legs must be straight and clean with good bone; the cannon bones short and the hocks well let down.

Show points for ponies are not just fads but, taken as a whole, are designed to provide a picture of a powerful yet well-proportioned animal, capable of speed and endurance while carrying the weight of a rider on its back. That is the basis of conformation, which receives fifty per cent of points from a judge looking at a class of riding ponies, while the remaining fifty per cent is divided between manners and suitability for a child to ride. Obviously, grooming and turn-out play an important part as well, because no judge will give a second glance to a dirty pony and a scruffy rider.

Grooming for the show-ring

While it is no good spending a few days before a show trying to polish up a neglected pony, much can be done in addition to normal grooming and care to present the animal at its very best in the show-ring.

Washing is a controversial subject, but in hot weather most ponies enjoy and feel refreshed after a bath just as much as we do, and, at least partial, washing may be essential for light-coloured animals such as greys and creams. Most people wash the mane and tail before a show, and the legs of ponies with white stockings or socks. It is largely a matter of common sense, which means that you do not wash a pony on a cold sunless day or leave it dripping wet to become chilled.

Special shampoos are sold for horses and ponies, so use one of these, as soap is difficult to rinse out of the coat properly and detergents are bad for the skin. A large sponge is essential for the job—the type made for car-washing is suitable—and several large buckets of warm water. If a pony has not been washed before it may be alarmed at first, but if you begin gently, chatting as you go, it will soon calm down.

Begin with the mane, squeezing the wet sponge out to soak it down to the roots and then add shampoo to make a good lather which can be rubbed in with the fingers. Guard the pony's eyes when you do the forelock. Rinse out thoroughly using the sponge while pouring clean warm water over the mane from a handy-sized bowl, until every trace of shampoo is removed. Brush the mane with a dandy or body brush and use a sweat-scraper on the neck, before wiping over with a clean dry cloth.

Do the tail next. Some written descriptions of tail-washing suggest that you place the tail in a bucket of warm water which is brought up under the dock as far as possible. Then, holding the bucket with one hand, you shampoo the tail thoroughly and rinse it in clean water, making sure that the root of the tail is both clean and free of shampoo, which will otherwise dry out to appear like scurf. This is all correct, except that holding even a light plastic bucket containing enough water for the purpose is going to be much too heavy for one hand. It is more practical to recruit an assistant for this job, who can hold the bucket while you have both hands free to wash and rinse the tail properly, which should be shaken to remove surplus water and then brushed out.

The whole or other parts of the body can be washed in the same manner, but remember to dry the heels carefully if the legs are washed, as neglecting this may result in sore, cracked heels. Even on a very hot day, walk the pony about until it is thoroughly dry.

A heavy mane or an untidy tail may need pulling to improve a pony's appearance. Do this when the animal is warm after exercise, as the pores are open and the hair will come out easily. Hairs from the mane should be taken from underneath, a few at a time with a quick snatch near the roots—try this out on your own hair to see how much or how little it hurts! Very thick manes should be pulled in several sessions, and not all at once, for the pony's comfort. Pull the tail where it is bushy near the root so that it flows away from a compact top, and remove any longer straggly hairs that spoil the general shape. It is best to let an expert show you how to do this properly; if you hurt the pony the first time it will be nervous when you have to try again.

While many people prefer a 'natural' switch tail, a banged tail looks very smart cut straight across about level with the hocks. To achieve this, raise the tail slightly by putting your hand under the dock while an assistant with a pair of sharp scissors cuts the hair to the required length. Leave the hairs a little shorter nearest the legs, which will mean that the end hangs level when the tail is carried normally. The shape of a tail can be improved with a tail bandage, but never use one wet as it can shrink and become dangerously tight. The tail bandage is fairly simple to fit with a little practice. When you have brushed out the tail, dampen it slightly with water and then fold the tail bandage round the tail near the top,

113

Pulled mane   Plaited mane

Left: Pulling the mane with a comb.

Below left, and below: Plaiting the mane in preparation for a show.

Bottom picture: Neat trimming with blunted scissors allows the headcollar to lie flat.

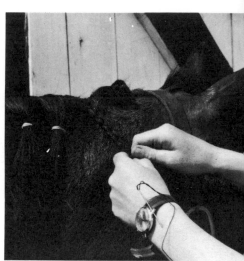

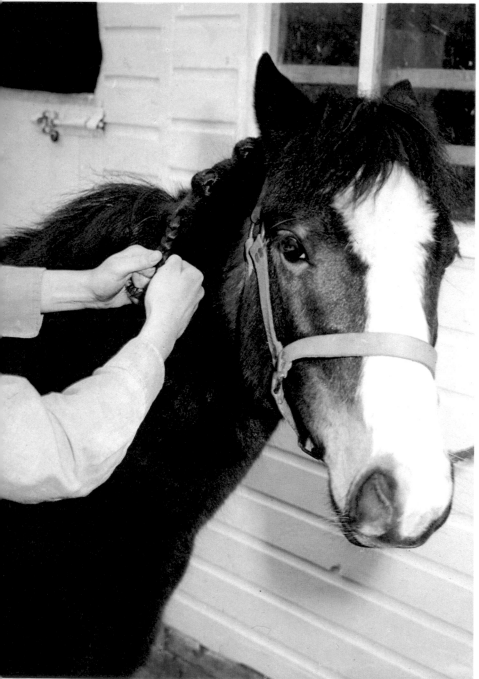

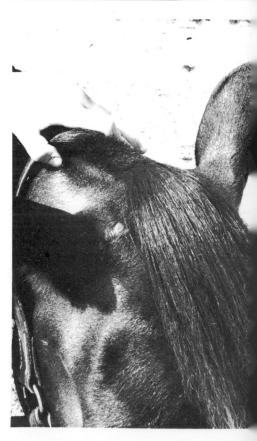

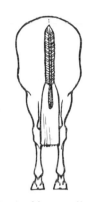

Pulled switch tail.   Plaited bang tail.   Fitting the tail bandage correctly is important for the pony's comfort.

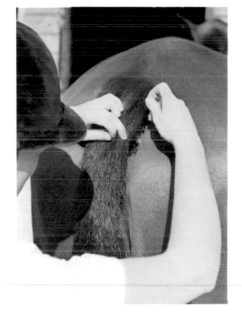

Above: Pulling the tail by hand from the top. This needs to be taught by an expert or the pony's tail will get very sore.

Right: Here we see the tail being plaited, quite a difficult task. A plaited tail is not pulled beforehand, but simply brushed smooth.

leaving one end free. Continue to wrap the bandage round the tail and fold the loose end down at the second fold, wrapping it into the bandage. Bandage firmly, but not too tightly otherwise the pony will be uncomfortable, almost to the base of the dock (the bony part of the tail) and halfway up again. Then tie the tapes in a neat bow.

This work can be done a day or two before the show, but the mane must be plaited on the morning of the show because it would be liable to come undone overnight and leave you with the problem of sorting it out all over again. Manes must be plaited for the show-ring (with few exceptions) and can make all the difference to a pony's appearance.

At one time seven plaits were the rule, six on the neck and the seventh being the forelock; but now any number are permissible and sometimes depend on the shape of a pony's neck, as several small plaits tend to make a thick neck look thinner, while fewer have the opposite effect when this is required.

Assuming that the pony has been groomed to a high gloss and the tail brushed and bandaged to keep its shape, plaiting can begin. First brush the mane with a damp water brush and then divide it into however many plaits you intend to make. Plait two-thirds of each hank of hairs, binding the ends tightly with strong cotton of a colour to match the mane, leaving two ends of cotton hanging loose from each plait. Then take a blunt darning needle, thread two loose ends of cotton through the eye, roll up the plait by turning the end under until it is tight against the roots of the hair and sew it into place, finishing off with a knot and snipping spare cotton with scissors. This process is repeated until all the plaits are made, including the forelock.

Remember to leave a space behind the ears where the headpiece of the bridle lies. The mane should be trimmed to allow the bridle to sit comfortably over the poll. Sometimes a mane grows down on the withers, and if these are of good shape you can trim off a little. Alternatively, make an extra plait but carry this one on to the tip, bind it neatly, and let it hang instead of being rolled and sewn. Plaiting is not easy at first but comes with practice.

Plaiting a tail is much more difficult and looks nice only if it is done with a professional finish. A well-brushed, pulled tail is usually preferable on a pony.

Tack for a show pony must be in good order and given an extra polish. A snaffle bridle is best for the novice pony, with a double bridle for the proper show pony, and a coloured brow-band can be fitted on these occasions to give a finishing touch—which may be enhanced if the rider wears a *small* button-hole to match, such as a rosebud or cornflower.

Your own clothes are important, because you must be neat and tidy just as much as the pony. Summer-weight jodhpurs are preferred, as these are more easily cleaned and pressed; a shirt of any colour except white is out of place and the tie should be plain and dark (or the tie of your Pony Club), held down by a gold pin fastened crossways for safety. Your jacket can be tweed for smaller shows, but ought to be navy-blue at a big show, and, in either case, remember to

116

Rider and pony dressed and ready for a show.

do up all the buttons because casual dressing can lose marks. Jodhpur boots should be worn and, obviously, a velvet cap. Gloves are sometimes forgotten but ought to be worn. They can be of white or yellow string, or pigskin. A riding stick should be carried, either blackthorn or with a sewn leather covering, which is held in the middle, usually in the right hand. The British Show Pony Society regulations do not allow a whip exceeding 30in (76cm), and an entrant wearing spurs will be disqualified.

You will need to take several items of equipment to the show, so put all these together so that nothing is forgotten. These are: a *clean bucket;* a *sponge* and other *grooming tools; needle, thread* and *scissors* in case a plait needs repair; *hoof oil* and a small tin of *Vaseline;* a *haynet;* and, in uncertain weather, a *rug* for the pony. A

117

clothes brush and a *comb* for your hair should not be forgotten. Wear jeans over your jodhpurs until the last minute to keep them clean. Then you are ready for an exciting day.

Showing a ridden pony

It is very difficult to remain outwardly calm on the morning of a show, when your pony and all your work in training and caring for it will be paraded before the eyes of a judge. But it is most important to do so, because if you are flustered you will infect the pony with nerves and then neither of you will make the best of yourselves. It is helpful to plan the day in advance, setting off from home punctually so as to allow plenty of time for the journey, and to 'warm up' and brush over the pony before you need to go to the collecting ring.

The warming-up process involves exercise that will get the pony moving freely, and gives you time to persuade your pony that, in the midst of all the noise and bustle, it must concentrate on working obediently just as it does in the home paddock: standing, walking, trotting and cantering at your command; reining back calmly and straight, and altogether behaving in the proper manner. This may require ten minutes or half an hour, and you must decide on the time needed and allow for it. But do not overdo it and end with the pony in a sweat.

Next comes the final polish. Go over the pony with a body brush, check that the plaits are tight, brush out the tail and if it is banged see that there are no stray hairs. Put a little Vaseline on a finger and wipe this round the eyes and nostrils to give them an extra shine, and wipe over the hooves with oil. Some exhibitors get an all-over gloss on a bay, brown or black pony by putting a few drops of liquid paraffin oil on their hands, rubbing them together and then smoothing down the pony's coat, including the tail. This can be effective but, overdone, might spoil an otherwise well-groomed animal. Avoid any grease or oil on any part of the body if the showground is dry and dusty.

When the time comes to go to the collecting ring, make sure that your number is tied on tidily and the right way up! Say a few words to the pony of a reassuring sort, because once in the ring you must be quiet and dependent on the aids for mutual contact. Make up your mind whether you wish to enter the ring first, last or somewhere in the middle, when the class is called and place yourself suitably in the line according to this decision.

It is a universal custom to enter the ring at a walk and circle to the left. The judge stands in the centre accompanied by one steward who checks the numbers against the catalogue of entries (and issues the prizes), and the ring steward who conveys the wishes of the judge to the competitors. Be aware of the ring steward at all times so that you are ready to trot on and canter at his command. Keep a suitable distance between yourself and fellow riders, but if the pony in front is slower than yours and spoiling your natural pace it is permissible to pass it. A judge is liable to keep a large class trotting for some time, as this is the pace at

A ridden pony being led in hand at a local gymkhana.

Left: Ready for the show-ring. An alert rider with a well-turned-out pony will catch the judge's eye.

Below: Ponies in a ridden class circle the ring under the direction of the ring steward.

which most faults are clearly seen, so get your pony going freely at a speed that suits it best, with one eye on the ring steward all the time.

If, hopefully, he calls you in to the front row you are on the way to a prize of some sort if you can put on a show that pleases the judge, who has already picked out your pony as one that moves well. Choose a place in the line with plenty of room between you and the other riders, keeping away from the one above you and, if necessary, politely asking the one below you to move down a little – otherwise never talk to other riders in the ring.

This is a moment when the rider and, consequently, the pony can lose concentration. It is all too common to see a rider slumped in the saddle while the pony has a quick nap during the time when a judge is looking at a particular entrant further up the line, but at any moment he may glance towards you to find a comparison, and if you and your pony are alert this will stick in his mind.

Riders near the top of the class will be asked to give an individual show, which should be a brief display of your pony's manners and your ability to ride it. This means the walk, trot, canter including a simple change of leg, a short gallop, rein-back, and halt. Choose a place in the ring where you are in full view of the judge and have room to execute a circle or figure of eight without tight cornering, keeping your show within the limits of what you know your pony will do well. It is wise to rein-back sideways on to the judge, in case it is not quite straight, and when you stop in front of him be sure that your pony halts and stands well.

When other riders have completed their shows, the judge will want to see the ponies stripped, so be ready for this by taking off the saddle, wiping over the saddle patch to remove any sweat marks and taking the reins over the pony's head. You should then stand in front, facing the pony and see that it is standing out well. When your turn comes, the judge will want to see the pony walk away and trot back, going steadily beside you without pulling back or cavorting sideways. Walk close to the pony, near its shoulder, so that you are in complete control of its movements. Then return to the line, saddle-up and remount.

Below, left: A judge takes notes as he moves along the line of ponies at a local show. It is important to teach your pony to stand still and not to fidget.

Below: A line-up of working hunter ponies, smartly turned out with their riders alert and interested.

At this stage the judge is likely to have selected the winners, but may ask for a final view of the ponies walking in a small circle before giving a decision. While concentrating on keeping your pony looking at its best, remember to watch the judge and the steward so that if you are called in for a place you will not miss the signal.

Since there can be only one first-prize winner and three or four minor places in a class, there are bound to be several disappointed riders and you may be among them. But hide your sorrow and look forward to another day, because bad losers look ridiculous.

Show-jumping

Opposite: Other competitors relax and let their ponies graze while a pony jumps with style over a practice fence.

Below: A confident jump over a staircase fence.

Show-jumping in Britain, with few exceptions, is governed by the rules of the British Show Jumping Association, which is based at the National Equestrian

Above: Debbie Johnsey clears a spread fence.

Above, right: Lindsay Vaughan on another good pony, Nutcracker.

Centre, Stoneleigh, Kenilworth, Warwickshire, CV8 2LR and has area representatives all over Britain who keep in touch with show organizers. There are a number of rules and these must be studied by competitors, since they cover a wide range, including correct riding clothes, the length of whip, permitted types of martingale, spurs, and behaviour in and out of the ring.

Ponies entered in competitions under these rules must be registered with the Association, and re-registered each year so that their Grading can be altered according to successes in the preceding year. A pony is generally the property of an adult member and ridden by a junior member of the BSJA.

The types of jump or fence used in the ring are well known to anyone who has watched show-jumping, and these are usually of a design approved by the Association. They advise that jumps should be strong and solid, but capable of being knocked down, and appear bright and attractive to competitors and spectators alike, except in working-pony classes where they are 'natural'. The height and spread of fences are also detailed, and the suitable speed for a certain course.

Internationally the sport of riding, including show-jumping, is governed by the Fédération Equestre Internationale at Avenue Hamoir 38, 1180 Brussels, Belgium, which issues rules similar in most respects to those of the BSJA.

In order to be successful in show-jumping, the first essential is a pony in the peak of condition, well schooled and obedient, yet full of courage and confidence. Schooling ensures that it does not rush its fences but takes off at a point directed by the rider, clearing the jump with the least effort and going on at the required pace. Show-jumping is not an art that a novice can learn alone, and the advice of a qualified teacher is important, so that you understand how to regulate the stride of your pony and its take-off point in relation to a given type of fence and to the distance between fences. Nervousness and uncertainty result in refusals, running out, or propping and bucking over in a scramble. A pony should enjoy jumping to be any good at it.

When you enter a jumping competition the pony should be well groomed and

124

turned out, although a plaited mane is not compulsory; you must wear the same clothes described for showing. There will be a practice area with a few jumps in a part of the show field near the ring, where you can warm up the pony and get it into the right frame of mind to jump freely in the ring when your turn comes. When it does, forget the spectators and concentrate on keeping your pony going, placing it carefully at each jump, and restraining too much speed without losing impulsion—both of you must remember all that you have learned and practised at home.

Above, left: A junior rider clears a very senior fence, and (*right*) Debbie Johnsey again. This time she is riding Nosey Parker when she won at Chepstow at the age of ten, and *overleaf* she rides in an adult competition on her horse, Assam.

Hunter trials

Hunts and Pony Clubs organize trials every season over a course which is as near as possible typical hunting country, and these are fun to enter besides making

Debbie Johnsey on Sea Gem jumps with plenty of room to spare in a novice class.

good training grounds for show-jumping and eventing. The course is of between one and two miles (1.5–3km), with about twelve fences, including hedges and banks and timber jumps, marked with red flags on the right and white on the left, and wide enough to allow two competitors to jump abreast.

A time limit is set for the course, with penalties for exceeding this. Penalties are also given for lack of control and behaviour likely to endanger followers of hounds, but the main list involves the hazards of the course resulting in: knocking down a fence, 10 faults; falling, 20 faults; failing to shut a gate or slip rail, 10 faults; first refusal, 15 faults; second or subsequent refusal on the course, 30 faults; third refusal, elimination; and you are also eliminated for taking a wrong course.

Your first attempt at a hunter trial will be made easier for you and your pony if you enter a pairs class with an experienced friend, as this will enable you to gain confidence. The important point to remember is that it *is* a trial, so never try to win at your pony's expense, but rather 'nurse' it round the course until you have gained experience.

One-day events

A one-day event is a shortened version of a horse trial or three-day event, usually organized by the local Pony Club, with three phases involving dressage, a cross-country course, and show-jumping. Clearly, none of the phases are as testing as those required at a bigger event but, nevertheless, they do demand precise schooling and riding.

The alternative name for eventing, combined training, is a good description of these competitions, since it is the all-round pony which wins by performing simple dressage, going on to cover a cross-country course with courage and speed, and then returning to the ring, still obedient and supple enough for a short display of accurate show-jumping.

128

A Pony Club member of the Fife team jumping an inviting cross-country fence in the
Pony Club one-day event championship.

Opposite, top: The Normandy Bank at the Badminton Horse Trials.

Opposite, below: A smooth turn at the corner during a combined training dressage test.

Above: A good take-off over a timber fence on a hunter trials course.

8 The world of the working pony

Show classes for ponies usually include one for working ponies, which, in this context, means a pony that is hunted regularly. Winners at larger shows may qualify for the the working Hunter Pony Championships held each year under the auspices of the British Show Pony Society; an organization like the BSJA which lays down rules and regulations for adult and junior showing members.

This is an example of the changing role of the pony, once kept as a maid-of-all-work earning a hard living but now a companion of our leisure time and a treasured possession. This is largely true but there are exceptions. A few pit ponies still work underground in British mines, not an ideal life for an animal, although nowadays they receive the best possible care and are a source of pride to the miners who look after them.

The growing popularity of riding has led to the establishment of a large number of schools. About 2,000 are licensed in Britain under the Riding School Act to keep an estimated 20,000 horses and ponies, which are inspected by local government officials to ensure a reasonable standard of care. This system is backed up and improved upon by horse and pony organizations, who add or withhold their own seals of approval. The majority of these schools teach how to ride adequately for ordinary purposes, but a few specialize in advanced equitation and provide accommodation for riders with their own ponies, so that they can learn together.

Trekking centres are increasing in numbers to provide an alternative to conventional holidays, and cater for children and adults who ride out every day on sturdy ponies, such as the Fell, Highland and Haflingers, to follow trails at a walking pace through rugged scenery, away from traffic and the so-called 'rat race' of modern urban living. Information on trekking holidays can be obtained from tourist boards, the British Horse Society or the Equestrian Federation of Australia. These holidays often encourage people to take up riding when they go home.

Horses and ponies have played a part in public spectacles since the days of Roman chariot races, and are the foundation of any modern circus – particularly since educated people are now less inclined to be amused by the unnatural antics of wild animals in the ring. Acts vary from tiny Shetland ponies performing

Opposite: Ponies being ridden bareback – a break from the normal riding school routine.

132

Above: Ponies working for their living. Pony-trekking holidays can provide the perfect setting for riding in beautiful countryside.

The two circus pictures show liberty horses taking a bow (*left*) and a Shetland act, which ends with the smaller pony standing on the larger, directed by Jasmin Smart, granddaughter of the famous circus owner.

A Lipizzaner stallion of the Spanish Riding School performs a *capriole*, the most difficult and dramatic of springs into the air.

tricks, often in company with dogs, to liberty horses controlled as a group by the ring-master, and ridden Lipizzaner stallions performing versions of the Haute Ecole movements developed at the Spanish Riding School in Vienna. Piebald and skewbald ponies were always popular for circus work but, since the spotted breeds are found in various sizes including the Knabstrup from Denmark and the Appaloosa of North America (both small spotted horses), these have a special appeal to the general public and are becoming more common.

A comparatively new role for the pony is in the field of riding for the disabled.

136

Top: A spastic boy leaves his wheelchair to enjoy learning
to ride with a local branch of Riding for the Disabled,
assisted by voluntary helpers.

Above: A pit pony hauls a light truck through the mine
tunnels. Only a handful still work in the mines, and they
are well looked after by the miners who take a pride in
their charges.

Right: A Highland pony still plays an active part in the life
of its native Scotland.

This skewbald pony works for its living by pulling a caravan in Ireland.

This idea began in Scandinavia a few years ago and was taken up in other parts of the world as an important form of therapy for people normally confined to a wheel-chair. Now many schools for the disabled keep their own ponies, and voluntary groups have been formed locally in association with livery stables to give basic lessons in riding within their capabilities to spastic and other disabled children, who not only find this great fun but often benefit physically. In Britain regional groups can be found by contacting the Riding for the Disabled Association at the National Equestrian Centre.

Ponies are still used as draught and pack animals in the remote or mountainous areas that remain without mechanized transport, and they often have to survive conditions of drudgery and neglect that, in the past, laid the foundations of strength and stamina – the hall-mark of British mountain and moorland ponies today. However, more and more are being bred with attention to points and temperament to find a place in the world of gymkhanas and the show-ring.

9 Other equestrian sports

There are a number of sports and games connected with horses. Some, like polo, are team games for their own sake, while others, such as mediaeval jousting and modern horse trials are practical tests for both horse and rider.

Polo

The game of polo is probably the oldest mounted game, dating from about 500 BC when it was played in Persia. In the course of centuries it travelled to Assam and

A polo match played against the backdrop of the mountains of Minnesota in America.

A fine back-handed stroke during the final of the Smith's Lawn Cup, Windsor. A good polo pony possesses speed, stamina, great agility and good response to the rider's aids.

notably to the state of Manipur, where a breed of pony was developed for the game – probably from Mongolian and Arab stock. The 10th Hussars introduced polo to England in the mid-1800s, and the Hurlingham Club was formed to lay down rules governing play. In succeeding years it was taken up in the United States and in the Argentine, and is now played in Australia, New Zealand, France and other places. Horses used for polo are always described as ponies because in the early days that is what they were; the Manipur breed being about 13 hands. Height restrictions were later removed and the modern polo pony is often a smaller Thoroughbred of suitable type.

A polo ground generally measures 900ft by 600ft (274m by 183m) and has a pair of goal posts at either end. There are four players on each side; two forwards, one halfback and one back, each player marking his opposite number. There is no goalkeeper and no off-side rule. The ball is made of bamboo or willow root, and the polo sticks, or mallets, of either malacca (stiff type) or whangee (whippy) with heads of bamboo root or persimmon. The shaft of a stick is about 51in (130cm) in length.

The game is played at tremendous speed and is divided into periods of about seven minutes (chukkas) in a total playing time of an hour; the ponies being changed after each chukka. While the objective is to score goals, this is

140

complicated by a system of handicaps, based on individual players and their teams' past performances. This may be up to ten goals for a player and forty for a team, and has an obvious bearing on the result.

Polocrosse

This version of polo was devised in Australia, where it has become very popular both with players and spectators. It may be described as a mixture of polo, lacrosse and basket-ball; played with a stick consisting of a polo shaft ending in a squash-racket head fitted with a loose net in which the ball is carried. The ball is rubber and about 4in (10cm) in diameter. A team comprises six players divided into two sections, who play alternate chukkas of eight minutes; each section consists of 1. 'Attack', 2. 'Centre' and 3. 'Defence'. A polocrosse ground is smaller

An energetic game of polocrosse at Sydney Royal Easter Show in Australia.

than a polo ground with the same goal posts, but has a 30yard (27m) line at either end over which only No. 1 of the attacking side and No. 3 of the defending side can play. In front of each goal there is an 11yard (9m) semi-circle and a goal cannot be scored from inside this area. The object of the game is to pick up or catch the ball in the net and throw it from one player to another, or gallop with it, until 'Attack' is in possession of it in the goal-scoring area and able to throw a goal. Both men and women play this game, which demands considerable skill.

Rodeos

Various events are scheduled in a rodeo, which is a sport based on aspects of work on a cattle ranch and so involves riding unbroken horses, cutting out single animals from a herd, roping calves, and so on. It is very popular in the United States and in Australia, requiring as it does considerable skill from the competitors, who risk life and limb trying to remain on the backs of gyrating mounts, and it makes an exciting spectacle for the crowds who come to watch. However, it is not a sport that appeals to everyone, because a horse is often forced to buck wildly by means of a cinch-strap, drawn very tight over the loins and under the belly, which inflicts a degree of pain on an animal – whether horse or bull.

141

Rodeos in Britain are very small-scale affairs, generally held in country districts where moorland ponies live semi-wild until rounded up for the end of summer sales, when some of the tougher types are entered in local rodeos organized by Young Farmers' Clubs and the like.

Opposite and above: The colourful parade Western-style is followed by a display of saddle-bronc riding at the rodeo.

Horse trials

Cavalry regiments have held horse trials of some kind for centuries past in order to prove the suitability of a horse in battle, but the first civilian trial held in Britain was at Badminton in Gloucestershire in 1949, the year after the first post-war Olympic Games. Since then, horse trials have gained wide popularity as a spectacle, perhaps due to television coverage and the interest shown by the Royal Family. The two most important venues in Britain are Badminton, the seat of the Duke of Beaufort, and at the home of the Marquess of Exeter, Burghley House near Stamford in Lincolnshire. The European Horse Trials are held annually in various parts of Europe and have both national teams and individual entries in the same way as the Olympic Games.

The major Horse Trials cover three days, hence the alternative name Three-Day Event, and are designed to test the obedience, courage and stamina of a horse, and the skill and fortitude of its rider. Of the three days, these comprise first, dressage; second, endurance in three phases; and third, show-jumping.

The rules of dressage training have been laid down by the Fédération Equestre Internationale and are based on the principle that after a course of progressive training a horse will be better balanced, putting less strain on itself; supple with improved paces, head carriage and general bearing; and utterly obedient to the aids applied by its rider.

143

Above: Richard Meade in the show-jumping phase of an international three-day event.

Below: H.R.H. The Princess Anne performing an excellent dressage test.

Above: A dramatic leap over the ditch during the cross-country phase – one of the most gruelling parts of eventing – at the Badminton Horse Trials which are held every year in April.

Endurance riding at a Horse Trial involves riding over roads and tracks, then a steeplechase course and the final cross-country course. This day is a severe test for both horse and rider and the cross-country phase is completed only by horses that are prepared to face and jump any obstacle.

The show-jumping on the third day proves that a horse is still fit, in spite of the rigours of the day before, and is able and willing to negotiate artificial jumps successfully in the show-ring. Constant veterinary checks are made throughout the trials to ensure that a horse is fit to continue. Points are gained each day to arrive at a total at the end of the show-jumping phase which will decide the winner and minor places. These combined tests represent the ultimate in all-round equine achievement.

Hunting

The term hunting is used in Britain to mean following hounds in pursuit of a fox, stag or hare; fox-hunting being considered the most important with over two hundred packs in the country supported by an estimated 50,000 people. Years ago numerous packs were privately run by land-owners but today the majority are governed by a committee consisting of the Master, a Secretary, Treasurer and, often, a Field Master whose job it is to control the mounted followers (who are known collectively as 'the field').

Hounds meet at a prearranged place, often outside an inn or at a crossroads, and sometimes at a 'lawn meet' – that is, by invitation at a private house where the host provides refreshments. The season begins on or about 1 November and ends in mid-April when the female fox (vixen) has her cubs. However, since the

All in a day's hunting. It takes a bold partnership to stay with hounds over this sort of country.

Right: The water jump provides a great deal of excitement at the three-day event. These two pictures show the rider approaching the water over a timber fence and the jump-out at the other side.

Opposite: A solid cross-country obstacle at the Badminton Horse Trials.

days of the Greek general Xenophon, about 400 BC, it has been a rule that to qualify as a sport the quarry must have a sporting chance of escape, and it is partly for this reason that the hounds are taken out cub-hunting a month or so before the real season begins. These are more or less informal occasions, usually beginning in September after the harvest is in, designed to teach young hounds their work and to instil into the minds of now-mature fox cubs a sense of danger and the necessity of learning lines of flight which, more often than not, will take them to safety.

A foxhound pack consists of a varying number of hounds hunting on a given day, not the total number kept at the kennels. Thus, according to the huntsman's decisions, you may hunt with a bitch pack, a dog pack or a mixed pack, which are always counted in couples – for example, a pack of 25 hounds would be described as 12½ couples.

There are a great deal of tradition and rules of etiquette attached to hunting. Correct clothes are important, varying in the degree of elegance according to whether it is a farmers' hunt or a grand one. Men can wear a scarlet coat, by invitation of the Master only, with white breeches, a white stock with a gold pin, black boots with mahogany tops and a silk top-hat; or the same but with a black

A private pack of hounds with the Master, assembling before the meet in the foothills of the Blue Ridge Mountains of Virginia.

or dark grey coat and a red or check waistcoat, or a black or tweed coat with fawn or brick-red breeches (black boots with black and brown with tweed) and a black bowler hat. Women wear a black, navy-blue or dark-grey hunting jacket, breeches, black bowler or hunting cap, a stock with safety-pin and black boots. Children can wear the same coloured jackets as women, with a collar and tie, and a hunting cap. Some wear tweeds and jodhpurs; this is usually permissible at younger ages and is certainly the most suitable clothing for novice riders. However, it is wrong to wear ties or pins bearing horses or foxes, masks, or to fit a coloured brow-band on a bridle.

Attending a meet for the first time may be an alarming prospect but common sense will carry you through. The important points to remember are: allow plenty of time to get there, riding to the meet at about six miles an hour (approximately 9km) so that the pony has lost its initial bounce but is still fresh; keep on the outskirts of the crowd with the pony facing the hounds to ensure that it does not kick one; and, when the field moves off, stay with a group of people who appear to know what they are doing. Obviously, the best way to learn about hunting is to go in company with experienced friends, and to go first to a special Pony Club meet where you will be taught the rules of hunting.

Lastly, remember that the privilege of hunting has to be paid for, either by an annual subscription which falls due on 1 May or by contributing to 'the cap' which is taken round at the meet. This money goes towards the substantial sums needed to pay the hunt servants and feed its horses throughout the year.

Driving

In recent years driving has become very popular as a competition event requiring considerable skill. A variety of small vehicles are used, including gigs, phaetons and dog carts, often drawn by Fell, Welsh and Shetland ponies, either singly or in pairs. A course is laid out with pairs of markers to represent gateways at intervals, and the object is to drive between them at speed without knocking over the markers. Points are gained for fast time and lost for every marker touched.

There is no doubt that it is much easier to control a ridden horse than a driven one, because in the first case you are there with the animal with all the aids at your disposal, whereas the driver is in only remote control and dependent on the reins, whip and voice. It is well worth visiting some of the bigger shows to see a driving class in action and to watch the artistry involved in guiding a pair of ponies between obstacles while they are trotting flat-out.

Driving is now recognized as a sport under rules laid down by the FEI, covering pairs and four-in-hands in events similar to horse trials, involving dressage, cross-country phases and obstacle courses.

Harness-racing has never caught on in Britain but is well-known as a sport in the United States and other parts of the world. The horses used are trained either as Trotters or Pacers, the former having a normal gait and the latter an amble –

A handsome turnout of pony and carriage, all ready for showing.

First past the finishing post in a trotting race on the Vincennes track in France.

150

that is, the legs move laterally, the fore and hind on the same side together which gives the impression of running rather than trotting. They are put to very light vehicles known as 'sulkies', consisting of two wheels with an arched axle on which a small seat is fixed. The driver perches on this with his feet on the shafts at either side of the horse's quarters.

Endurance riding

While officially recorded long-distance rides are a comparatively new form of sport, isolated efforts have been made for several centuries, generally as the result

Above: A team of five Shetland ponies about to enter a driving show class.

Overleaf: Part of a three-day driving event – a team of Irish Hunters are driven skilfully round a turn in one of the obstacles on the course.

151

Riders on the Golden Horseshoe long-distance ride, held each September. To enter the Golden Horseshoe, riders and horses must qualify at one of the shorter rides held throughout the spring and summer months, organized by the British Horse Society. All types and breeds of horses are eligible, including crosses with the larger native ponies – the Connemara, Highland and New Forest.

of wagers and involving considerable cruelty to the horses taking part, many of them dying during or after these marathons. Nowadays, however, endurance riding is properly organized with strict veterinary supervision, and is becoming increasingly popular in the United States and Australia, and, to a lesser extent, in Britain where the Golden Horseshoe Ride is held annually over a course of seventy-five miles (120km) to be covered in two days.

The most famous endurance ride in America is the Tevis Cup. This is held in July each year and covers 100 miles (160km) of terrain between Tahoe City and Auburn, California. The route traverses the Sierra Nevada, crosses rivers, and passes through forests and canyons and along mountain trails. The time allowed is twenty-four hours but there have been records of less than thirteen hours. Entries in major endurance rides are restricted to horses that have completed successfully in less arduous qualifying rides and are at least five years old and a minimum of 14 hands high.

In Australia several endurance rides take place each year, but the most testing is the Quilty Cup, which is held in September over 100 miles (160 km) of rugged hill country in the Blue Mountains near Sydney.

Glossary of common terms

Above the bit The pony carries its head too high so that the bit operates on the corners of the lips instead of the bars of the mouth.

Action Movements at all paces. Good action is light and effortless, not plodding. At the walk the hind foot should, at least, cover the print left on the ground by the forefoot. The pony must go straight, the hind foot following the forefoot in the same line.

Aids Means of conveying instructions to a pony. The natural aids are voice, hands, legs and body; artificial aids include whips, spurs, martingales, etc.

Arab The oldest of the world's recognized breeds and one that has had the greatest influence on the world's horse population. Its characteristic qualities are stamina, conformation, soundness, courage and speed.

Behind the bit The pony evades the bit by tucking its nose towards the chest, becoming 'overbent', and thereby dropping the bit.

Cast A term used to describe a pony that has rolled violently in the stable and lies on its back with all four legs in the air, unable to get back on to its feet. See page 54 for advice on what to do if this should happen.

Cob This term refers to a strong, stocky animal, large in the body with powerful, short legs – a sturdy and reliable mount. See page 21 for a description of the Welsh Cob.

Collection A pony is collected when its head is raised, bent at the poll, jaws relaxed, with supple quarters and hind legs engaged.

Colt Young male pony, ungelded.

Conformation A pony that is in proportion throughout, making a balanced whole (see pages 111-12 and 60 for 'Points of the Horse').

Counter-canter An exercise to achieve suppleness and balance. It involves cantering on a curve, to both left and right, with this sequence of legs: inside leg, outside hind and inside fore together, with the outside fore taking the last step.

Crib-biting Stable vice, usually due to boredom, in which pony chews any available timber in its stable. Bad for teeth and can cause colic.

Eel-stripe Dark stripe from crest to tail. Otherwise dorsal stripe. Usual in dun ponies.

Filly Young female pony.

Flexion The flexible movement of the head from the poll, in which the pony's jaw is relaxed and without strain.

Foal Young pony under a year old. Filly foal, colt foal.

Frog V-shaped cushion on sole of foot.

Green Part-trained pony in need of further education.

Horse-box Vehicle with compartments to carry several animals; generally fitted with side and/or rear loading ramps.

In-hand Show classes for led ponies as distinct from saddle classes.

Loose-box Stable in which a pony is not normally tied up.

Made The opposite to 'green'. An educated pony.

Martingale Straps fitted to the noseband or reins at one end and to the girth at the other. They are designed to lower the horse's head and increase the rider's control. They need to be fitted with care and should not be necessary for a pony.

'Mealy' markings Pale, flecked colouring round the eyes and muzzle of Exmoor ponies.

Mouth A good mouth answers to a light hand. A hard mouth has been rendered insensitive by bad riding or excessively severe bitting.

Mucking out Cleaning out dung and soiled bedding from stable.

Near-side Left-hand side of pony. The side from which a rider usually mounts.

Off-side The right-hand side of a pony.

On the bit The pony holds the bit lightly in its mouth, accepting it willingly at all paces with no sign of resistance.

Over-faced Asking a pony to jump beyond its capacity.

Quartering Grooming.

Rising In context of age: pony of 5½ years is described as rising 6.

Sheltie Tiresome nickname for Shetland pony.

Slug Lazy or disheartened pony; not one out of condition or sick.

Staring coat When the hair is rough and lacks healthy gloss. Indicates illness.

Straight mover A desirable quality. When viewed from front or rear the pony's legs move in two straight lines.

Suspension The moment at the trot and the canter when the pony is suspended with all four legs in the air.

Tack Saddlery.

Thoroughbred Essentially a racehorse, the English Thoroughbred is descended from three Arabian sires imported into England in the late seventeenth and early eighteenth centuries. It is frequently crossed with native breeds to add quality.

'Toad' eye The prominent eye of an Exmoor pony.

Transition This means a change from one pace to another. In training the pony, all transitions should be progressive, moving from halt, walk, trot through to canter and back again to halt.

Tucked-up Loins drawn up: indicates under-feeding, over-work or sickness.

Weaving Stable vice (see crib-biting). Pony sways from side to side.

Wind-sucking Pony gulps down air with clenched teeth. Like weaving and crib biting, it is a boredom-induced stable vice, which can cause colic.

Index

Page numbers in *italic* refer to the
illustrations and their captions.